C Programming Proverbs and Quick Reference

Ron Wodaski

PUBLISHING

A Division of Prentice Hall Computer Publishing
11711 North College, Carmel, Indiana 46032 USA

This book is dedicated to my wife, Donna Brown.

Publisher
Richard K. Swadley

Managing Editor
Neweleen A. Trebnik

Acquisitions Editor
Gregory Croy

Development Editor
Stacy Hiquet

Production Editor
Tad Ringo

Editors
*Cheri Clark, Grant Fairchild,
Gayle Johnson*

Editorial Coordinators
Rebecca S. Freeman, Bill Whitmer

Editorial Assistants
Rosemarie Graham, Lori Kelley

Technical Editor
Bruce Graves

Cover Designer
George Harris

Production Director
Jeff Valler

Production Manager
Corinne Walls

Imprint Manager
Matthew Morrill

Book Designer
Michele Laseau

Production Analyst
Mary Beth Wakefield

**Proofreading/Indexing
Coordinator**
Joelynn Gifford

Indexer
Loren Malloy

Production
*Terri Edwards, Mark Enochs, Tim Groeling, John Kane, Carrie Keesling, Juli Pavey,
Michelle Self, Kelli Widdifield, Allan Wimmer, Phil Worthington*

Overview

Programming Proverbs

C Quick Reference

Table of Contents

Programming Proverbs

19 Functions   255

Acknowledgments

I owe the biggest debt of gratitude to my wife, Donna, whose support was essential to getting this book completed. I literally couldn't have done it without her.

I would also like to thank Gary Wisniewski of Apex Software in Pittsburgh. Gary is a truly gifted and skilled C programmer whose contributions included reviewing the manuscript, articulating the concept of library-based control of the design better than I ever could have, and supplying the basis for the Programmer's Checklist.

A tip of the hat also goes to those CompuServe junkies who supplied me with their wit, ideas, and criticism as I was writing the book. Chat on, dudes!

Trademarks

About the Author

Ron Wodaski hails from Wilkes-Barre, Pennsylvania, and is a graduate of King's College in Wilkes-Barre. Originally a journalist, he started getting programming experience in the early days of personal computers when he designed and wrote custom software using BASIC and dBASE II on his Osborne. Since that time, he has graduated to C and has been both a programmer and a project manager for various companies. His varied roles have included testing at the former Ashton-Tate, managing a test laboratory, serving as Systems and Programming Manager for several companies, and developing a never-released C API for dBASE. He currently writes books on a variety of computer subjects, pens the occasional science fiction piece, and writes documentation in the fields of software and robotics. When last heard from, he was writing a book on Windows and Multimedia for Prentice Hall Computer Publishing, due out at the end of 1992.

Programming
Proverbs

I

Introduction

When I first began learning C, I was quite dismayed. It seemed so simple, and yet so complex. I wondered if I would ever grasp the language.

It wasn't until I realized that C was a *real* language that I began to make significant progress programming with it. Because it is so subtle, C can be as expressive as any other language—not just any other computer language, but any *language.*

C'est bien ça, oui?

"That's just it." Looks a heck of a lot better in French, doesn't it? The heart of the matter is that C is a very *expressive* language. Used well, it not only performs as planned, but it communicates to others both our purpose and the means used to achieve it.

Which brings me to the central theme of programming: maintenance. A lot of what you see here has to do with the assumption that someone else is going to have to read your code. The truth is, even going back to your own code a month later is a lot like reading someone else's code. We all learn, our techniques evolve, and going back to what we did last year, last month, even last week can give us a serious case of the willies. Of course, the fact that half of the cost of a programming project goes into maintenance is probably an important consideration, too.

Everything about coding, from good algorithms to elegant one-line masterpieces, has two goals: the immediate task that the code was designed to perform, and the less obvious task of communication.

C programming is evolving. Some would say that we are in the midst of a full-blown revolution, called *object-oriented programming* (OOP). Many of the concepts of OOP—objects themselves, inheritance, encapsulation—are built on the same concepts that make for good "plain vanilla" C programming. This book is not about OOP or C++; it is about C and how to use C most effectively.

There is an excellent reference book for writers, written by the poet Robert Graves. The title is *The Reader Over Your Shoulder.*

The main thrust of the book is that all writers should imagine, as they write, that there is a knowledgeable, interested reader looking over their shoulder. This act of imagining the reader in concrete, immediate terms is valuable to writers. It helps them think of their audience without resorting to useless abstractions.

As programmers, we can benefit from something similar. *The Programmer Over Your Shoulder* doesn't have the same catchy ring, but it is an important concept. If you can imagine someone standing or sitting next to you while you code, you will find yourself writing code that is just a little bit better organized, just a little bit clearer in design, and just a little bit easier to understand.

Who is this programmer? Yours can be whomever you like. Mine calls himself Clarence.

Clarence has some stellar qualities for the job he does. First of all, he is interested in what I'm doing. He has a habit of gently interrupting and asking pertinent questions. He's not too proud to cluck at me now and again for taking the easy way out, and I get a smug sense of satisfaction when I know that Clarence approves of what I've done.

I highly recommend the serendipitous approach to selecting the identity of the programmer over your shoulder (who would otherwise have to go around as the POYS). Natasha, Poindexter, Helen, or Aloyisous Alexander Needlemeyer III—don't settle on a name until you know it's right.

So whether it be considerations of design, execution, or testing, the underlying theme of the book you hold in your hands is this: C is a *language* first, and machine code second. I have yet to see this approach result in problems. On the contrary, the extra time spent up front invariably results in fewer bugs, faster walk-throughs, shorter testing periods, and easier maintenance down the road.

But enough *hurler à la lune* (howling at the moon); let's get practical!

1

Principles of Program Design

1

Old Programmer's Proverb: The more time you spend up front on design, the fewer mind-destroying changes you'll have to make later.

Old Programmer's Corollary: In the real world, the design is never finished.

It's one thing to recite homilies about good programming practices, but it's another thing entirely to put them into use on a daily basis. You've heard about the ideal way to design a program, but you've also faced tight schedules and major changes that squeeze the schedule even tighter. Even when time is in short supply, there are ways of going about the business of programming that help you stay organized and on top of things.

Libraries

One of the best ways to organize your design is by using libraries. As you will see, libraries offer a flexible way to code. They can provide overall control over the design while still providing enough room to resolve the details of implementation.

Technically, a library is nothing more than related chunks of code—groups of functions that serve some basic purpose. Libraries can do a lot more, however, if you are willing to be disciplined about how you put them together.

Let's take a look at some of the fundamental issues involved in program design. Then you will see how properly constructed libraries can help.

There are two fundamentally different ways to create a program. Not to get too technical, they are the following:

♦ Top-down

♦ Bottom-up

Each has advantages and disadvantages. In recent years, top-down programming has received all the good press, but it might not be the best way to go.

1

Top-Down Programming

The idea behind top-down programming is to start with an overall design and then program to that design. In other words, decide up front what the program will do, and then write code to make it do just that.

The advantages are that you know ahead of time what needs to be done, so you can set up responsibilities and schedules and regularly evaluate progress. Even if changes need to be made (don't they always?), the existence of a plan helps everything come together.

The disadvantage is that it is never possible to anticipate everything. Sometimes the things you don't anticipate can require major changes. If you have any doubts about the weaknesses of top-down design, read *The Soul of the New Machine* by Tracy Kidder (Avon Books, 1990).

Top-down design lends itself to the typical corporate structure because, despite its flaws, it does allow for a certain amount of compartmentalization and organization. These can be valuable attributes when administrative folks need to be kept informed about things such as current progress and variations from the original design.

Bottom-Up Programming

I once had a project director who was fond of throwing out a particular saying at meetings when people started to talk about the complexity of a project. He would call attention to himself— discreetly, with a cough or by turning in his seat—and then mutter, "This isn't rocket science." What he meant was that anyone could do it.

I later came across an E-mail exchange that made me look at that idea from another point of view. The project director was also saying that rocket science was complex, difficult, and only for the best of the best. In fact, the way rocket science has been conducted is a model of bottom-up design.

1

"Rocket science" was a real nuts-and-bolts effort. It worked like this: the rocket guys would sit around and talk about what might work. Then they would sit down and try to build what they had thought of. More often than not, they had a hard time building it; when they could build it, it wouldn't run; and when it did run, it blew up before it did what it was supposed to do.

Doesn't that sound a lot like the way programming works in the real world? More often than not, you have a hard time coding it; when you do code it, it won't run; and when it does run, it blows up before it does what it's supposed to do. In other words, bottom-up design is just another way of saying "by trial and error."

You can dig out some simple programming gems from such efforts.

Tip: Don't be afraid to make mistakes.

Mistakes are the tuition in the school of life. I once forgot to insert a limiting number in a program. As a result, $26,000 worth of inventory was reshipped to the same customers, who now had two of everything they'd ordered from us. I remember the long walk to the president's office after that one, expecting to get fired. The meeting was short and sweet. He looked at me for a moment, and then said, "It costs about $7,000 a year to send someone to college. I just paid for your four-year degree. I hope it was worth it." That was all. I didn't have the nerve to tell him that he was still $2,000 shy of the full tuition, but maybe he expected me to cover it.

Tip: Learn from your mistakes.

In other words, don't waste your tuition. Making the same mistake twice is a clear signal to everyone that your tuition costs are double what they should be.

At the very least, every mistake tells you one thing—how *not* to do something. Often, your mistake also contains hints about what will work. Mistakes are valuable, and too often they are overlooked as a part of the programming process.

Mistakes are also the key to successful bottom-up programming:

Round 1: The task at hand might be a design document, or it might be a prototype. Everyone finds fault with it, but at least everyone is thinking. Maybe the whole thing is thrown away, but the general direction is now clear, even though you haven't addressed the details.

Round 2: The design or prototype is a better fit. Whole parts of it clearly fit into the overall project and can move forward. Other parts still need work; they're full of mistakes.

Round 3 and onward: The fit gets better and better. The details become clear, and coding begins in earnest. Confidence is high, because many of the mistakes and pitfalls have been identified.

Tip: *Don't get bogged down in the details too soon.*

One danger of bottom-up programming is that you can get lost in the details. One of the reasons people use top-down programming so much is that it feels safer. The problem, however, is that it's also more conservative, which can lead to stagnation and poorly written code.

Programming involves many unknowns. They range from the general (can we do this at all?) to the specific (how will I code this algorithm?). How you resolve these unknowns determine how successful the end result will be. One of the best ways to uncover and resolve unknowns is by prototyping; if there is a better way, I haven't seen it. Just creating a prototype, however, doesn't solve anything if it's approached incorrectly.

For example, I've seen too many prototypes that were put together just as marketing tools to sell the idea of a program. Much less often have I seen a prototype built to test a programming concept or idea. That's a real loss. Don't be afraid to do it all wrong, because you will learn a lot when you do. You don't have to spend a lot of time on a prototype. If you try to throw one together, however, and actually start to get your hands dirty, you will learn things about the task at hand that you never would have guessed were there.

1

If you are not willing, however, to start over if the prototype is wrong, you are heading for trouble. One of the things you should learn from a prototype is what kind of architecture will work—and the pasted-together architectures used in prototypes seldom qualify.

Tip: Set short-term goals that fit into a long-range plan.

Another danger of bottom-up programming is straying from the plan. If you are experimenting, you can wind up following dead ends or good ideas that don't have anything to do with the project at hand. Always relate your short-term assignment to the long-term plan. That's where libraries come in.

Libraries as a Programming Foundation

Creating and using libraries forces you to stay on track. It's practically automatic. The details on creating and using libraries are covered in the section titled "Layering."

It is critical to split your code into libraries; it forces a certain amount of organization into the process. However, you can't just arbitrarily divide the code into libraries. Each library has to have a reason to exist.

I've seen a lot of different ways to divide code, and only a few that worked. One major piece of software that just about everyone has used (names are omitted to protect the guilty) used the requirements of the testing department to divide the code into libraries. There were directories with more than 500 files in them. This is not how to divide code into libraries. But if you get confused about how to do it, at least now you know that some pretty important people in the field get confused, too.

A library provides a service. It is a collection of tools and code that uses these tools. The library may export tools to other libraries, but it doesn't have to.

Rule: *The absolute minimum of code passes between libraries.*

The interface consists of well-regulated functions that must meet strict criteria. (See the section titled "Layering.")

Anything can go on in a library, and some pretty frightful code has been known to occur there. As a programmer friend once told me, "Somewhere in the system you have to get dirty." Inside a library is the place to do it, but in the interface to the other libraries, stay clean, clean, clean.

Each library is like one rocket experiment. As long as it does what it's supposed to do, the rest of the project can be successful. How it does it can be less rigid.

It takes a lot of effort to make a good library structure work. However, the pain involved, while keen at times, results in gains that make it more than worth the effort required.

Modularity

If you are implementing a rough design on the fly, keeping track of what's what is one of the tougher tasks you face. The code seems to spring leaks, would-be functions hang out in the code, and you are never quite sure where the constants are declared.

What's a programmer to do? Modularize.

Libraries are, of course, modular by their nature; each library is a module, even though there may be many separate files in a library. To be effective, a library must be broken down into pieces that make sense. It's easy, though, to get bogged down in library administration. Every library that you ever saw had a librarian, right? To avoid that problem, you need some general rules to guide the creation and maintenance of libraries.

Tip: A good library always has a section for tools.

This is a lot like the reference section of a real library. The tools are for use only in the library; you can't check them out and take them somewhere else. These tools are like local variables: they are limited in scope. There are other kinds of tools that are exported: they are similar to global variables, but they have to respect

1

hierarchical relationships. See the section titled "Layering" later in this chapter for details on exported tools.

The tools section is just that—a section, a single piece of the library that should be dealt with as one thing. If you are writing a piece of code that you will use more than once, it belongs in the tools section and must follow the rules for tools.

Tip: Good programmers are always building and maintaining their tools.

Tools are the starting point of every decent library. But you are always learning, always finding new ways to do things, always finding new things to do. Like the overall design of a project, the design of your library will grow and change over its lifetime.

The ideal library is mostly self-maintaining—if you can follow some basic rules, that is.

Rule: Keep your tools simple.

The best tool is a simple tool. Simple, in this context, means that the tool should do one job, do it well, and do it quickly. You should be able to explain what a tool does in one sentence. It may take a lot more to explain *how* the tool functions, but the idea is to create tools that do one task.

If a tool tries to do too much, a couple of things can go wrong. First, it can be hard to remember what the tool is for the next time you need it. Second, the tool might be overly ambitious, and that leads to bugs and other troubles. Third, the tool might become too specialized and therefore not be as useful as it could be. A good example of this approach to tool building is the UNIX operating system—nearly the entire system is built out of tools.

Rule: Tools are reusable code.

Each tool is like a complete application because it must work under a variety of conditions. The best of your tools will be used by other programmers, and they will bring their own ideas to bear on it. Your tools should be robust enough to be used in a variety of situations.

The preceding two rules work with each other. A simple, well-designed tool is more likely to be reusable.

Rule: *Build big tools out of smaller tools.*

Small tools are best for "dirty" tasks. By "dirty" I mean things such as operating-system-specific calls or assembly language routines. If a tool is designed correctly, it can do what it has to on the inside without imposing a penalty on its callers, such as an inordinate number of parameters. The more parameters you pass around, the slower your code runs.

Another advantage to this approach has to do with changes. If your higher-level tools are built out of the low-level tools, you need to fix problems in only one place: the low-level tool that caused it. If you don't build your tools this way, you might find yourself having the same problems over and over.

Of course, if you change a calling sequence, you must go back and modify all the higher-level tools that call that low-level tool. Again, UNIX is an excellent example of building tools on top of other tools. This brings us to the next rule:

Rule: *Don't be afraid to make changes.*

A programmer friend of mine tells a story about a project on which he had design responsibility. Additionally, he was also responsible for the glue layer between the low-level stuff and the high-level stuff. His library was used by almost every other library in the system.

He wrote a function that, unfortunately, made an assumption that turned out to be false. That function returned the value of the current field in a database record. As the project went on, it became clear that a function was needed that would specify fields other than the current field. There were two possible courses of action:

◆ Write an additional function that took a field name or number as one of its arguments.

◆ Modify the existing function so that it handled both the general case and the current-field case.

1

The first course is easier. If a new function is created, everyone who needs to call something besides the current field could do so, and no one would need to change their existing code.

But consider the implications. First, that's one more piece of code to add to the executable. One little piece of code isn't much, but how many times will a similar decision get made, adding who knows how many "little pieces of code?" Second, these two possible courses represent different ways of handling the data. One represents a program in which the concept of "current field" has meaning. In the other, of course, the discipline of the idea of "current field" is lost.

If the new function were really needed, then the design was wrong. That's very different from the idea of a mere missing function. It becomes a question of keeping or not keeping a fundamental paradigm for data handling in the project: do you have a current field concept, do you toss it, or do you modify it somehow?

Rule: Every tool should fit into the overall design of the project.

In this case, the programmers put their heads together and decided that the concept of a current field was too limiting for what they were trying to do, so they asked my friend to modify his design. With the new design for field access, a function resulted that was neither the old one nor the one everyone had thought should replace it, but something that turned out to be better than either of them.

Everyone went back to their code, not merely to replace one function with another, but to implement a new data-handling design that would save time both in the remaining phases of development and in the execution time and code size. This brings us to the final tip:

Tip: Think globally, but act locally.

If you follow these rules, you will find that your libraries have an internal logic that actually makes it hard to create chaos. But these rules address only what's going on within a library. You will almost always have more than one library. Interlibrary relations are also important. You need to take your bottom-up organization a bit further if you are to truly create useful, dependable, functional libraries. That's what the next section is all about.

Layering

It's easy enough to see the benefits you get from modularizing, from breaking your code into small pieces. It's a kind of horizontal division, like cutting a pie into pieces. A piece is almost always more manageable than the whole pie. But horizontal division is just a part of the process.

Here is a rule that, if followed, automatically creates a layered relationship between libraries:

Rule: If library A calls library B, B must not call A.

Libraries always sit on top of one another. If you always follow this rule, you will find (later in the project, of course) that when you get around to drawing an architectural diagram, it will turn out as though the whole thing had been planned.

It's as simple as looking both ways before crossing the street. Before you finalize any part of a library—every tool, function, structure, module, and so on—make sure that it does not violate this rule.

You can look at it like building a chain: every link is connected to, at most, two other links. If you follow this rule, you will find that when you are done building the chain, it will be just what you expected.

The benefits of this approach include the following:

◆ The time spent on making sure the lower levels are right pays off when it is time to code the higher levels. Think of it as object-oriented programming without all the fuss and bother. (Of course, if you are already using OOP, it's not such a bother.)

♦ You will find that you have a much clearer idea of the structure and architecture than if you had glossed over this step.

I have worked on projects that used this technique, and I have worked on projects that did not. I can only say that when this rule was followed, every programmer on the team was able to contribute. When it wasn't, chaos ensued, and programmers found it hard to stay focused and write reliable code.

Maybe even more important was the ease with which new programmers could be brought up to speed. It's much easier to join a team whose tools you can comprehend than one whose tools aren't organized.

Programmers may indeed be doomed to reinvent the wheel, but I'd rather be reinventing at the level of McPherson suspensions than donkey-cart wheels.

The following illustration shows what a multi-layer architecture looks like. There are two obvious features: lumps and skinny places. The lumps are libraries and the skinny places are the interfaces between the libraries.

A good library exposes as little of itself to other libraries as possible. This lean approach maintains the architectural requirements between libraries, but it allows the author of a library a good deal of freedom at the same time. In practice, this balance usually works out to be about right. For special situations, it can be modified one way or the other, favoring more or less control as needed.

Data movement within a layer is very different from data movement between layers. Layers have secrets that must not be revealed to other layers.

For example, consider an application that must open files. If I write code to open a file, there are many issues to consider. Some are very specific, and some are quite general. A specific issue might be, "How do I tell the operating system that I want to see if a certain filename already exists?" A more general issue would be the whole concept of opening a file. I might want to set things up so

1

that I don't even care if it was a file that was opened—I might just want some data, and I might not care where it came from. I don't need to know about the structures that are used to keep track of operating-system-specific information such as file handles and buffers.

In other words, there are both low-level and high-level concerns when opening a file. The low-level concerns usually have to do with the mechanics of opening the file; the high-level concerns usually are specific to the application. In between are issues that are shaded toward one or the other.

Let's look more closely at a hypothetical file I/O example to show how a multi-level architecture can be implemented.

We'll work with three layers. A complex application might have more layers, but three is enough to illustrate the concepts. Keep in mind that layers are relative. An application that must work across a variety of platforms, or with a variety of data formats, probably will have more layers than one that does not.

In this example, the lowest layer is the hardware or operating-system interface. This layer knows some things the other layers don't, such as what operating system it is dealing with, and maybe what hardware it is running on. Functions at this level may be written in C or assembly language.

The middle layer can be viewed as a "glue" layer. It provides the link between the highest and lowest layers. It "knows" about the needs and requirements of both layers.

The highest layer might be called the "programmer interface" layer. It is completely ignorant of the issues of the lowest layer, and it is relatively intuitive to use.

Remember the rule stated earlier:

If library A calls library B, B must not call A.

This means that our high-level library can call the mid-level library, but the mid-level library cannot call the high-level library. Also, the mid-level library can call the low-level library, but the low-level library cannot call the mid-level library. It's a one-way street.

1

Let's build a simple set of file I/O functions to illustrate this point.

An Example of Layered Functions

Assume that you need to do the following things with files in a hypothetical application:

◆ Register a file user (so that you can get the associated permissions for reading and writing)

◆ Open a file with the appropriate permission level

◆ Close a file if it is open

◆ Read data (if the user has permission)

◆ Write data (if the user has permission)

You will need five functions to perform these higher-level tasks. Each has the prefix hl to indicate that it is at the highest level:

```
int hlUserHandle = RegisterUser(char * UserName,
                          unsigned int PermissonLevel)
int *LedgerHandle = hlOpenLedger(char * FileGroupName,
                                     int UserHandle)
void hlCloseFile(int LedgerHandle)
void hlGetBalanceDue(int LedgerHandle, double bal)
void hlUpdateBalanceDue(int LedgerHandle, double bal)
```

(Strictly speaking, some of these functions would be internal to the particular library doing these tasks. Those functions should have a prefix to indicate that, such as i for internal.)

Note that the hlOpenLedger function takes a file group name, not just a filename. The group name would be a ledger name, such as *Payroll* or *Accounts Payable*. The read and write functions—hlGetBalanceDue and hlUpdateBalanceDue—are special-purpose functions that read and write data without your knowing what files, fields, tables, and so on are involved.

The driving force behind the particular design you will use is the concept of the user and the associated permission level. The user is a high-level issue only. At the lower levels, the concerns are more mechanical: read permission, write permission. So when you build the functions for the high level, you will include the concept of a user. Conversely, the concept of user will be absent from the middle and lower levels. Neither of the other two levels has any reason to know anything about users, although the interface to the middle level might include a user as a parameter.

"Doesn't this violate the rule about isolating layers?" you might ask. Not at all.

From the higher-level viewpoint, yes, you are indeed passing something you view as a user to the lower level. But if you are clever, the way you represent the concept of the user will use some technique that the middle level also is aware of, but has nothing whatsoever to do with the user.

For example, if you use a pointer to a structure of user information to physically represent the concept of the user, isolation can be maintained. For example, at the higher level, you might pass a variable with a name like UserHandle to a middle-level function. However, the definition for the mid-level function might include a variable name like OpenMode to represent the same data. Your design must accommodate this kind of dual point of view to make the library concept work. This may seem trivial, but the concept is critical to good design.

Tip: The same data means different things to different layers.

In other words, each layer has its own concepts, which serve the purposes of that layer first and foremost. That gives programmers working in a specified library a great deal of freedom to get the work done without worrying about what they are doing to other libraries.

Rule: The tool portion of every library is divided into exactly two parts: internal tools and exported tools.

The internal tools can do what they please, how they please, so long as they do the job. There are no outside constraints. The only constraint is maintenance; the code you write must be maintainable by you or someone else in the future. Just because you get down and dirty here and there is no excuse to get sloppy. This part of the design is all yours—if it's your library.

1

The exported tools are a different story. Every parameter and every function name means something to someone outside of your library who uses it. Every facet of every tool has to make sense to someone who has no idea what is going on in the guts of your library.

However, if you can get this part of your library right—really *right*—you have a solid foundation on which to build.

Here's how to build a good export section for your library:

◆ *Names are everything.* When you name your functions and variables, you must be conscious not only of what you need the function to do, but of what others need it to do.

◆ *Be prepared to iterate.* As soon as you export something, you can expect others to come back and tell you how or why it doesn't meet their needs. You'll do the same to them, so it all works out.

◆ *Be prepared to be stubborn.* You want good reasons for making changes after an iteration or two. By that point, lots of folks are using your exports and depending on them. Don't make unnecessary changes. On the other hand, if you really need to make a change because the design isn't right, fight for what you know is right. Don't let a raft of moans and complaints stop you from making everyone change their code for the better.

◆ *Be prepared to be flexible.* You hear ideas about your functions, about how you've named them, about how they are organized, and about how some of them should go in other libraries. If you get a good suggestion, follow it.

Rule: *A library is a service, not a dictatorship.*

Your library is a small service business. Think like a capitalist: satisfy your customers. "The customer is always right." Well, not always, but often enough to make it worth listening to them.

Coding the Top Layer

You now know that a registered user has a permission level that controls access to the file for read/write operations. You need to write code with that in mind.

At the top level, these facts control the kind of information you see in the functions you are using. You can use names like UserName, PermissionLevel, GroupName, and so on. At the top level there is no need to have filenames as such. You work with names that are more in line with the concepts used at the top level. Instead of a filename, you might use things like AccountsReceivable, which might include half a dozen actual files. It depends on the implementation.

All you should see at the highest level is application-specific information. Therefore, all your file operations must use the high-level functions. Opening a file with a function at a lower level will almost certainly mess up the record-keeping, because the mid-level functions, which handle record-keeping, are out of the loop.

Let's take a look at what a high-level function might look like. (Note the use of mid-level functions using the prefix ml.)

```
LEDGER *hlOpenLedger(char * FileGroupName,
                     char * UserName)
{
        unsigned int PermissionLevel;
        /* Note the use of typedefs to differentiate
           pointers as to their purpose. */
        LEDGER *LedgerPtr;
        USER *UserHandle;

        /* Make sure the name exists. */
        mlVerifyFile(FileGroupName);
        /* Use an internal high-level function to get the
           handle associated with the user's name. */
        UserHandle = hlGetHandle(UserName);
        /* Use another internal high-level function to get
           the file open mode for the user. */
        PermissionLevel = hlGetPermission(UserHandle);
        /* Open the files. At the middle level, the
           permission level is really a file-open mode.
           Same data, different point of view. The type
           of LedgerPtr (LEDGER) is identical to the
```

```
        FINANCE_TABLE type. */
    LedgerPtr = mlTableOpen(FileGroupName,
                            PermissionLevel)
    /* Register the user of the filename.  You can
       assume that the mid-level function couldn't care
       less what the nature of the handle is.
       It just registers handles. */
    mlRegisterFileUse(LedgerPtr, UserHandle)
    /* Return the group handle. */
    Return LedgerPtr;
}
```

The mid-level functions "know" some things that the high-level functions don't. For example, the mid-level function `mlTableOpen` takes a parameter called `PermissionLevel`, but (unknown to the high level) this is really just a file open mode—read, write, append, and so on. At the high level, you did not need to know that the permission level controls the file open mode; this is taken care of for you. The mid-level function definition, however, makes no mention of permission levels, just file open modes. This enables each level to work with the concepts that are appropriate and useful for that level.

The name of the mid-level function—`mlTableOpen`—suggests that at some point there was a compromise in naming. The middle level knows about tables. And apparently there are high-level libraries somewhere that also know about tables, although your library doesn't. Therefore, the name reflects the more general case of TABLES, whereas in your library you work with LEDGERS. Somewhere, there are high-level libraries that use TABLES for something besides LEDGERS, such as maintaining information about vendors.

Isolating such things is one of the principal gains from multi-level architecture. It frees the programmer at each level to think in terms and concepts that are familiar, as well as appropriate, to the task at hand.

Coding the Lower Layers

Now let's look at the mid-level function that takes the next steps in opening the table.

```
/* The FINANCE_TABLE type is identical to the
   LEDGER type. */
FINANCE_TABLE *mlTableOpen(char * TableName, unsigned
                          int OpenMode)
{
    FINANCE_TABLE *TablePtr;
    FINANCE_FILE  *FilePtr;

    /* Create and fill a structure for the file info.
       The table will contain an entry for each file
       in the group. */
    TablePtr = mlCreateTableInfo(TableName);
    /* Get a pointer to the first file in the group. */
    while (FilePtr = mlGetNextFile(TablePtr)
    {
        /* Open one file. */
        llFileOpen(FilePtr, OpenMode);
        /* Put the file information in the structure.
           This is going to be either an OS-specific
           file handle, or a pointer to a file
           structure.
           This allows you to track the record position
           and so on. */
        mlStoreFileInfo(FilePtr, TablePtr);
    }
    /* Initialize relations among the files in the
       table. */
    mlInitTable(TablePtr);
    return(TablePtr);
}
```

This mid-level function uses one low-level function (note the
ll prefix) and several mid-level functions. The low-level function
(llFileOpen) opens one file at a time. Because it is a low-level
function, it is ignorant of things such as tables and table structures.
That is why you must call a mid-level function (mlStoreFileInfo)
for each file you open immediately afterwards. It stuffs the file
information into the table structure for later reference. At the
middle level, however, you do not need to worry about what that
low-level information is; you can just use the FilePtr as a
convenient handle with which to manipulate the files in your
table.

The llFileOpen function, however, must know all about the
operating system it uses to open the file. It can safely get its

1

figurative "hands" as "dirty" as necessary in order to get the job done.

There are other things going on here, however. This function first allocates space for a structure to contain information about the table. You pass the FileGroupName, so it is safe to assume that the function mlCreateTableInfo uses that name to find out what files need to be opened. It stuffs these filenames and space for file maintenance information into the structure and allocates enough memory for the structure. It returns a pointer to the structure so that you can easily use it again later.

The while loop opens one file at a time, as described in the preceding code. Each file has pertinent information stored in the table structure. You can assume that this includes things such as the operating-system-bestowed handle or structure pointer, and internal housekeeping information such as current file position. Note that only mid-level functions know about tables and table structures; your high-level library "thinks" in terms of ledgers.

After you have opened all the files and dutifully recorded information about each, you call a mid-level function (mlInitTable) that initializes your table, setting all required relations between the various files, opening indexes, and so on. You can assume that the information about how to do this is already recorded in the table structure, having been placed there during the call to mlCreateTableInfo. You do not need to worry about whether this information was recorded as constants in arrays, or loaded from a file, or whatever. Such things are quite properly hidden from you at this level. In OOP programming, this concept is called *encapsulation*.

Putting the Layers Together

A complete system would show how all the functions relate to one another and to the variables and structures that make up the data storage. There would also be other libraries at the high level using the functions exported by the middle layer. For example, there probably would be a vendor file (or table), and it would need to be opened. It would have different requirements, and therefore different data structures, would use different concepts, and so on. There isn't room to show all of that here, but I hope the basic points about a multi-level architecture are clear:

◆ Each layer isolates itself from all but the immediately adjoining layers.

◆ Knowledge is a one-way street. The lower level knows absolutely nothing about its callers.

◆ Platform-specific information is limited to the very lowest layer.

◆ A layer may call only the functions of its own layer and the layer immediately below.

◆ The top layer should deal strictly with intuitive concepts to make programming efficient and maintenance easier.

The last point should not be taken to mean that the lower levels do not need to work with intuitive concepts. It just means the following:

Tip: The highest level is defined by complete reliance on intuitive, rather than machine-based, concepts.

Wherever possible, you should create intuitive, easy-to-understand concepts at every level. Of course, the lower the level, the harder that can be.

Bottom-Up Example

Believe it or not, you've been working with bottom-up programming the whole time!

"Preposterous," you say. "You started at the highest level and worked your way down."

Well, you did stray from the strict bottom-up approach, but you can't just start at the bottom with no idea of what's happening around you. If you are going to work with the tools at the bottom of the hierarchy, you had better do so with a decent knowledge of what's going on around you.

What you have done is create a prototype. No code, other than what you saw, has been written. You have merely examined the relationships between the layers (and don't think I didn't adjust those relationships during the various drafts of the manuscript) and laid out a possible route to follow. The vast majority of the work remains to be done, and you can now start at the bottom—by building the various tools you know you will need at the lowest layer. You then can try them in the next layer up while you create the tools for that layer. If they work, great. If they don't, revise until they do.

Whatever system you use, many of the same problems must be dealt with. In top-down programming, conformance to the design is the controlling factor.

Tip: In bottom-up programming, experimentation drives the design all during the project.

The main reason that I urge bottom-up design is that there are so many unknowns in the programming process, and I think it's smart to acknowledge that up front. That means writing code that you know might change, based on a design that's imperfect but getting better and better. I like that better than thinking that I'm diverging more and more from the ideal.

Perhaps it's just a way of thinking. Perhaps the way you think has a great deal of influence on your success.

Interfaces

You have already had a good look at the internal interfaces in the code (between libraries). There are two more that you need to pay attention to: input and output.

Input: User Interfaces

1

By far the most difficult kind of input to code for is the user interface. Design issues predominate; the user interface has limited impact on the actual writing of code. Although the programming techniques for a windowed interface, for example, differ from a simple full-screen text interface, they still have a great deal in common. If the code is structured properly in both instances (adhering to the rules set forth earlier), you should have a good handle on the architecture either way.

The real problem with user interfaces is that they really need to be completely isolated from the mechanics of the code and the machine it runs on.

Today's graphical user interfaces (GUIs—oddly pronounced "gooies") go quite far with that concept. I love working in a windowed environment—most of the time.

But clearly there are times when beauty and simplicity are at war with each other. Some of the most useful interfaces between code and human are just plain simple. Even in a windowed environment, I prefer to keep a command line handy for humdrum tasks such as file copying.

Tip: Don't make assumptions about what the user wants, likes, or needs.

This is the One Great Rule of user interfaces. There are as many experts on the subject of user interfaces as there are programmers, designers, and system architects.

Here's a little war story. I once worked at a leading PC software house. The company's products had tremendous market penetration. Because it seems that the only way to grow is to enhance the products already out there, attention went to enhancing the user interface, inarguably the weakest part of the product—or so everyone thought.

Many people spent a great deal of time trying to decide the best way to enhance the user interface. Naturally, everyone had an

1

opinion. After several years of experimentation (during which time the market share eroded quite noticeably), a few designs stood out from the rest, at least as far as the company leadership was concerned.

The time came to spend some money on actually going ahead with one of these ideas. A decision was made and the money was spent. The enhancements were coded, and the resulting product was marketed with all sorts of fanfare.

It didn't sell very well, despite years of effort and tons of money.

What went wrong? In a nutshell, all the ideas for the enhanced user interface came from people too close to the product to know better. The people who really knew—those already using it—were hardly consulted at all.

This is a prime example of how *not* to design a user interface.

Users might never give a moment's thought to the ideal interface. In fact, they might not have a single constructive thing to say about how to design a user interface correctly, but they can tell you what's wrong.

It's your job to make it right. How do you do that?

◆ Make a list of what's wrong with the user interface. If there is no computer yet, make a list of what's wrong with the manual interface.

◆ Find some good examples of user interfaces that work and use them as a foundation. If the operating system supports user-interface features, consider the strengths and weaknesses of that support before moving on.

◆ Go over the list with appropriate users. Discuss the pros, cons, and costs of various kinds of solutions. Hash things out.

◆ Prepare a prototype design, either on paper or coded, and review it with users. Note their reactions to see whether you are on the right track. Make a list of what worked, what didn't, and why. Circulate it to the users.

1

◆ You are now well on the way through the iterative process of a good user interface. Ultimately the only advice worth beans on the subject is to keep at it until you get it right. The only experts on the user interface are the people who use it, and they have preconceptions and habits that limit their ability to design a new interface. Consider all those people using WordPerfect 5.1—it does not have a very friendly user interface, but it sells like hotcakes.

Ignore everyone who tells you differently. There are no secrets to interface design, no grand schemes that guarantee success, no universal architectures. Good user interfaces are as diverse as the applications that computers are put to, and as varied as the people who use them.

Data Interfaces

The user interface is a subset of all data interfaces. There are many kinds of data streams to deal with.

It's easy to criticize a poorly organized section of code. It's right there in front of you. All you have to do is look at it and say, "Yup, that's a piece of spaghetti, all right."

But the blame for the problem can sometimes lie elsewhere. A poorly designed, fragmented data interface gives a programmer precious little to work with. It's hard to write good code when data is flying at you from all directions. I've seen some pretty strange code result from this, and it's not (necessarily) the programmer's fault.

The links between code and the data interface are more complex than might seem to be the case. A number of issues are involved:

◆ Data structures (how big, how many?)

◆ Data flow up and down (you did remember to layer, right?)

◆ Data validation (when—now or later?)

1

- ◆ Data construction (roll your own data?)
- ◆ Passing data around (whose data is this, anyway?)

Structures

Data structures exist in a number of places besides your include files. They haunt the entire program, because they impose a way of looking at the data.

Tip: Isolate the data structures from the restrictions of the machine whenever possible.

Good code is the result of incorporating clear concepts about the application into the code. This extends to data structures as well as to lines of active code.

Include files are the place where these concepts are developed. If you can nail down a workable concept in the include files, the coding is easier. It can be as simple as the name you give your structures, and as complex as what data to include in what structures and whether to form a more perfect union with those structures.

Tip: Don't just throw data into structures and hope for the best. Group it for convenient reference.

Creating a windowing library? Fine. Think (again) in terms of layers. What's at the highest layer? Put it in one structure. Keep it simple.

What's in the next layer? Divide it into related groups, put each group in a structure, and put those structures in the high-level structure. Continue until you're done.

Data Flow

Moving data from the user interface into the depths of the program, and back out again, is not as trivial as it sounds.

Misunderstandings here are a major source of bugs. If you can't look at a piece of data and track it to its source or destination, you are in trouble.

Big chunks of data are okay to pass around (by pointer, of course) at the higher levels of the program. The higher levels are, by definition, the great collectors. It's a good indication of the success of your organization if you can successfully use such large structures.

But the reverse is also true. If you are passing structures with small, discrete amounts of data in them at the lower levels, your organization probably is efficient.

For example, your larger structures should contain pointers to smaller structures. When necessary, at the lower levels, you can pass just the smaller structure, thus hiding the irrelevant details from the lower levels.

Tip: Passing around big chunks of data at the lower levels is a good indicator that your design is still too rough.

Data Validation

You can validate it now, or you can validate it later.

Tip: Validate data as close to the point of input as possible.

This has a corollary that's obvious when you think about it:

Corollary: Don't validate until you have all the data needed for the validation.

Naturally, these tips are mutually exclusive.

Validating as close to data input as possible can get messy if you don't structure the process correctly. Your code can begin to look like the reject pile at a sausage factory.

Making the decision about where in the code to check for the error is nothing to gloss over. For example, handling a bad file

1

handle is easy when you write the code in terms of file handles, and impossible when the concept of file handles is buried in a lower layer.

Tip: Data entry and data validation are the same step.

They are not the same thing, but the same step. This means that the act of collecting data should be the act of validating it. From a code standpoint, a function that gets data is the same function that makes sure the data is valid. That means your code has one step for both processes.

Think of every data-gathering function as having the prefix GetandValidate:

```
GetandValidateName(buffer);
GetandValidateAddress(buffer);
```

This concept became prominent in the fourth-generation procedural language of many database products. It usually comes in the form of a function or clause that is part of the data entry procedure. The data entry procedure does not return data until it is validated.

Naturally, you will face situations where good data is not available, but something needs to be done with the data. The best choice usually is to simply redirect the data stream to a holding bin for sick, injured, or unperformed data. It is identical to the home for good data, but it leads nowhere. It's just a holding tank. At a later date, the data in the holding tank can re-enter the data stream *at the same point where it left.*

As with all general rules, there are plenty of exceptions. Try to make a conscious choice each time you respond to an error. There are three fundamental choices: terminate (with cleanup), correct, or set aside for later correction.

That gives you the conceptual framework for properly controlling data—which brings up, somewhat tangentially, the subject of data auditing.

Data Construction

Sometimes you have to make up your own data. This is a lot like indexing, so let's take a moment to consider indexing.

An index enables you to access data in some order. The index does not rearrange the data to do this. An index is a collection of pointers to the data, and it is only the pointers that are arranged in the desired order. These pointers are constructed by looking at *keys* in the database. A key is some part of a record (often a single field, such as LASTNAME) on which we want to sort.

The science of indexing includes the art of programming fast, compact indexes. There are already numerous schemes for doing this, and most of them are available off-the-shelf to suit a wide variety of situations, but you can't construct a good index key by buying one. There is an art to it.

Tip: *No matter what you've heard before, the only good key is a unique key.*

There are plenty of indexing schemes that do not require a unique key. They are, in fact, practical to use in various situations.

I wish, however, that there was another word for it besides indexing. Real indexing is done with unique keys. I'll use the word *sort* to indicate that data is organized according to some rule, and that the rule might not use a unique key.

Why the emphasis on unique keys? Control. In financial applications, for example, one extraneous, unaccounted-for piece of data can throw the whole system out of whack. Thus, unique keys are needed. A unique key says that two pieces of data cannot occupy the same piece of memory or disk real estate.

When you must create an audit trail in a program, you need to assemble packets of data that point back to the real data. The only way to do this unambiguously is with unique keys. The audit file may contain many, many records pointing to just one thing, and the unique key makes certain of that.

1

You can ignore the foregoing if you're just throwing together a mailing list database for your Aunt Tessie; otherwise, ignore it at your own risk.

What would Clarence (the programmer over my shoulder) say if he ever found out?

Parameter Passing

Parameters are the heart of C. Because C was implemented as a language that relies heavily on functions, there are many functions in your code. The number of parameters these functions use is mind-numbing in its extent.

Good naming conventions are essential. This topic is discussed in more detail in Chapter 2, "Documenting Your Code," in the section titled "Examples of Good Naming Conventions."

There is a small war going on in most programs between the locals and the globals. The general rule—we've all heard it—is the following:

Dubious Rule: Globals are bad; locals are good.

This usually is true, but don't forget that there is a class of data for which the opposite is true.

Tip: If an item of data is in widespread use, global is good and local is bad.

Some things are just meant to be used by everybody, and you want to make sure that they wind up as globals. To do otherwise weakens your code and slows things down. For complex data structures, passing pointers is normally more effective than using globals.

And don't give me a whole lot of static over it, either, because statics are fine, too. They are baby globals.

Output

1

When I wrote my first commercial programs, the first thing I did was ask folks what they wanted as output. I didn't know where I should start, and that seemed as good a place as any. After a few years of programming, I realized that there were some other important things to do before sitting down to write the code. But you could do a lot worse than to start with the end rather than the beginning.

Part of the reason for this is blindingly obvious. If you want to build a house, it helps to know up front whether you want a two-story or a ranch. Likewise, if you are writing a reporting program, it helps to know up front whether you want the output to go to the screen or the printer.

But there's more to it than that.

Every item of data in a report or on a screen has to come from somewhere. If you have a good grasp of what must come out, you can make sure that it goes in somewhere. It can be very frustrating to discover well into the process that the user wants something out of the back end that you never knew about. More than once, I've had to redesign software to allow for one measly morsel of data.

Tip: What comes out must go in.

Here is an example. I was designing a system to keep track of seating at an event. It seemed pretty straightforward: each table could seat ten people, and people got assigned to a table when they paid for their ticket. So I plunged in, and was I ever deceived by the apparent simplicity! In the real world, people like to sit next to each other, but they don't always buy their tickets together. I had made no allowance for storing information about seating preferences. The user was not happy.

So I had to dig back in. Not only did I have to add the capability to store information about seating preferences, but I had to write code that would handle things such as moving people from table to table, conflicting preferences, late payments, single

1

seats left over—you name it! I felt pretty crazy by the time it was working, all because I had failed to do one thing at the start: ask the user what output he wanted, instead of what I thought it should be. What did I know?

Tip: Ask, and don't assume anything.

Algorithms

When I first listed this topic, I knew it was important to talk about, but now that I'm writing about it, it's hard to know where to begin. Looking back on algorithms I've known, it seems that each one presented unique problems and required a lot of careful thinking.

Tip: Good algorithms run deep.

A good algorithm is a lot like a good performance: there's a lot more there than is visible to the untrained eye. A figure skater, for example, practices for untold hours to perfect things that seem impossible to you and me—triple axels, triple sow chows, and other permutations of human motion that are more like fantasy than reality.

Why does the athlete practice so much? At first glance, you might think it is simply a matter of repetition, and, at some level, that's probably true. Repetition, however, gives you the opportunity to do something you can't do any other way. It gives you a chance to really get to know the subtle details of what you are doing, to study the nuances of an activity.

You can't do that if you don't force yourself to pay attention to something you've already seen or done a thousand times.

Tip: A good algorithm results when you force yourself to learn something from every single iteration of the implementation.

So even if every algorithm requires a unique solution, you can find a better solution if you pay attention. It's not easy to do; going over the same code again and again is just plain boring. It is not inherently stimulating. It is not motivating. You have to motivate yourself, with questions such as

1

"What is hidden here that I've never noticed before?"

"What can I learn about the process that is not yet reflected in the code?"

"What questions haven't I asked yet about the process?"

Sometimes, it's just a matter of telling yourself to get ready, the same way a performer gets ready back stage. Anticipate learning. Anticipate excitement. Tell yourself there's more here than meets the eye, and challenge yourself to find it.

In other words, go ahead and make a mountain out of that molehill.

2

Documenting Your Code

2

Are you one of those programmers who just loves to sit back and document what you've done? Or are you a mere mortal who wants to get back to the *real* work as soon as possible? Well, you're in fine company. Programming feels like progress (well, most of the time). Documenting is like sitting still, going nowhere. So why bother, right?

Hey, don't look to me for justification on that one! If you think that documentation is a waste of time, get a ruler and slap your knuckles. Then read on.

Rule: Documentation is the key ingredient in a program. It unlocks the power inherent in the code.

Suppose you've written code that does exactly what was intended. Suppose it has zero bugs. Suppose everyone is thrilled with it; suppose you get a raise, maybe even a promotion. (Hey, why not?)

Now suppose that the requirements change. Suppose you aren't there, and the code is not well-documented. What happens? It's not hard to predict. Someone else is going to moan and groan when he sees what you've left behind. That someone is going to spend a lot of time figuring out what's going on in the code.

That same someone is also going to have to rewrite some of the best of your code, simply because he can't figure it out. The rewrite probably will cost time to write/test/debug, and it won't ever be as good as what you did, because the new guy can't integrate it well unless he understands what you did originally! The client or user is going to be frustrated because it's taking so long—not to mention the person who monitors the budget.

You could say that you wrote a good program, but you'd have a hard time convincing me it was good code, because it did only part of its job. It did what the user wanted it to, but it didn't communicate to the next programmer down the line.

I'll fall back on the time-honored computer/car analogy. Have you ever tried to troubleshoot a car's electrical system without an electrical diagram? If you have, you know how

2

frustrating it is. You have no idea which wire leads where, because all the wires disappear into a hole somewhere. It takes an enormous amount of time to troubleshoot under those conditions. The only good thing is that, if you wanted to, you could always plop down the $20 for the electrical diagram and end the misery. But if the documentation isn't there, what do you do?

> *Tip: Insufficient documentation is the leading cause of baldness and stomach ulcers among programmers.*

Just kidding, of course.

> *Real tip: Document your code while imagining the next programmer looking over your shoulder.*

Talk to this imaginary programmer. Explain things to him. Pretend he is interested in what you have to say, that he needs the information to maintain your code. Someday there will, in fact, be a programmer in exactly that position. It could even be you.

Documentation Levels

Coding has begun. You are writing one or more modules that have a defined input, process, and output (thanks to the excellent specification you've prepared, at least for your own corner of the project). The code is excellent, of course—you're writing it, right? But what about the documentation? There are five levels of documentation.

> *Project level:* The documentation includes the specification, any technical documents prepared during production, and the final user documentation. Normally, none of this documentation is located inside any of the code. It is all external, because it is generally concerned with the project or program as a whole. For my purposes, I'll be looking at just the specification.

> *Module level:* The documentation can be either internal to the code or external. I prefer to see module-level documentation inside the module. However, programs are available

2

that can extract it from each module, collate it, and print it for viewing as a whole. The danger with external documentation is that it almost always gets out of sync with the code.

Function level: Each discrete function should have its own documentation. The format is not important, but it should include parameters, return values, side effects, possible errors and error codes, author, and revision date.

In-line documentation: Sometimes, despite your best intentions, the code itself is not enough to communicate what is going on. If that's the case, you can include comments right in the code.

Naming documentation: The names you give to variables, structures, functions, modules, and so on are part of the documentation. They are not just reminders to you. They are communication tools above all else.

The Specification

The specification is the first documentation that exists for most software. Of course, in many situations, the spec is nothing more than a gleam in the architect's eye. This is a shame, because the time saved in not writing a specification is a mere fraction of the time wasted later when there is no spec for everyone to focus on.

Examine the penalties one pays for lack of a spec:

◆ Without a spec, everyone is free to have his own idea of what the final product will do and be.

◆ Without a spec, it is easy to be unclear about your responsibility to the project.

◆ Without a spec, you might not know when you are done.

◆ Without a spec, it is easy to change in midstream, confusing everyone concerned.

◆ Without a spec, it is hard to change things effectively. What are you changing from? How large is the change? What will it cost?

Even when I do a one-man project, I do a spec—because there is no such thing as a one-man project. Besides me, there is always at least one other person: the client or user. If I have a spec, we can both look at it and decide whether it describes what we want. If it doesn't, we can change it until it does.

Tip: Don't start coding the final product until you have a signed, sealed, and delivered spec in your hands.

However, keep this in mind: The spec only describes what you know at the time you write it down. It is inherently incomplete. Top-down programming relies heavily on the spec, whereas bottom-up programming considers it only as a basis for creating a prototype.

Now that I've given you the hard line on writing a spec, you can turn your attention to the problem of writing a good one.

Tip: Be specific.

Don't speak in generalities. If you're going to put a name on the screen, don't just say, "Name on the screen." Are you going to use titles? Are titles optional or required? Are you going to store the name in one field, or will you store each part of the name in different fields? How will the name be listed on reports? On what reports is this particular name required? Are there other names? How do they differ? How are they the same? Where does the data for the name come from? What processing will be done with it? What other parts of the program use it as a resource? Where does it end up? What intermediate steps are required or optional? How trustworthy is the source? What kind of validation will be required? Knowing these kinds of things in advance takes a huge load off the programmer's back.

Tip: Don't stop asking questions until you don't have any more questions.

Tip: If you find another question, ask it.

2

I can't prove it, but from my experience it appears that every hour spent writing a decent spec cuts at least an hour from the coding time. Someone is always pushing to see code written, but it does no one any good to start writing code until the person understands what the code is supposed to do.

Rule: Prototyping is another form of specification.

In other words, go ahead and code early, as long as you realize that it's only a prototype. By prototype, I mean something whose code is totally expendable. Not "first draft." Not "something we can build on." The only good prototype is one you are prepared to throw away completely. Not that you necessarily will. You might find that your prototype is wonderful, and build on it. But unless you are prepared to throw it all away, you won't take the risks that make a prototype so useful. So think of your prototype as just another part of the spec that happens to involve some coding.

Library Documentation

A good library is more or less self-documenting. The key to a good library lies in its structure, not in the documentation. If the library is well-structured, you can document it as effectively graphically as you can with words. Here are the key elements of good library documentation:

◆ Functions that are exported to other libraries should all be in one header file that is well-documented. See the following section for information about well-documented functions.

◆ The change history is accessible in one place. This can happen either because you put it in one place or because you have a tool that collects it and puts it in one place.

◆ There exists a flow diagram of the library's functionality and relation to other parts of the system.

Module Documentation

2

First, I'll define what a module is.

Definition: A module is a single file that contains one or more functions.

At the top of every module, you need to tell everyone what the module is about. In most cases, you also keep the change control information there, but because schemes for change control vary, that is not absolutely necessary.

Tip: At the top of every module, document only things that involve the module as a whole.

I know this tip seems obvious, but it's so easy not to follow this advice. You wind up either leaving out things or trying to include too much. Neither approach is helpful.

You are going to document each function, so you don't need to do that here. You grouped the functions in this module for a reason, so state that reason and move on.

I recommend the following minimum documentation at the top of a module:

◆ *Description:* Tell what the module's purpose is. Be concise but complete.

◆ *Technical issues:* Who can call the functions in this module? Is it exported or local to its library? Are there any restrictions on its use? How complete is it? Does it have any unimplemented functionality?

◆ *Modification history:* If you make a change, document it—not in shorthand no one but you will understand, but in clear, concise English that Clarence can readily understand.

That's really all that is required—a brief description that enables someone to understand why the module is there in the first place, technical information that enables the next programmer to grasp usage issues quickly, and a history of what you have done.

2

Function Names as Documentation

So, what's the best way to document a function?

> *Tip: The name of a function or tool is the best documentation you're going to find for it.*

There are two kinds of function names: sentence-like constructions (typical of large libraries with many similar functions) and compact conglomerations (typical of frequently used functions and smaller libraries).

Compact function names are best for functions that are commonly used. The standard C library is full of such names. Commonly used functions that you write should also use this approach. If you are writing a database application, the name of the function used to get data from a field probably will be short: `GetField`, `GetFld`, or something similar.

I prefer sentence-like names, but programmers differ strongly on this point. I don't mind the extra typing, because I like the extra ease upon rereading my own code later. In addition, sentence-like names are much more closely matched to the task that the tool performs. When you use a name like this, C makes the leap from a *programming* language to a *real* language. Someone reading the code can get a good sense of what is going on. Face it—in-line comments are helpful, but if you rely on them too heavily, the code is still hard to read. You are reading the comments, not the code!

This is a subject on which Clarence is outspoken. He likes code that embodies clear concepts, not just neatness. Names embody the concepts, so good names create good code. *Quod erat demonstrandum.*

> *Tip: To name a function well, you must understand it well.*

Functions are the lowest level that requires documentation. In addition to giving a function a good name, you should include the following items with each function in the file where it resides:

2

◆ *Description:* In plain English, tell what this function does. Keep the jargon to a minimum so that even if I don't know the details of the application, I still will have a pretty good idea of what the function does.

◆ *Parameter documentation:* In plain English, tell what each parameter is and how it is used in the function. The second part—how it is used—often is overlooked. If I'm going to use your function, I want to know why you included all those parameters.

◆ *Return value:* Document what you are sending back to the caller. Also include information about any error-specific return values.

◆ *Side effects:* Does the function change any globals or statics? Does it write data to the disk? Does it alter the contents of a structure? Does it change the state of anything? Document it!

That's it. If you use intelligent naming conventions, you don't need any more than that at the function level. You can document change history at the module level.

Functions in Header Files

There are only two kinds of header files: local and exported. Each library can have one or the other or both.

The local header files should have a convention for naming which makes it clear that the functions in it are local. I like *i* for internal because it stands out, but you can use your imagination.

Exported functions need a header file of their own because that is the mechanism used to export them. Anyone who has a legal right to the functions can access them by including the header file.

The functions in the export header file need some special attention:

◆ Make sure the names are clear, even to someone who doesn't understand the nuances of your library.

2

◆ Include a prefix unique to your library (see the section titled "Names as Documentation").

◆ Use sensible, self-contained variable names for all parameters. Be just as careful and consistent as you are with the function names. Using the right parameter names can save repeated trips into the source's code to find out what the function does. Clarence smiles when I use good parameter names, and I like to make Clarence happy.

◆ Be consistent in your abbreviations and other naming practices. If you use the word get in one place, then use it everywhere; don't mix metaphors.

The export header file is the most compact distillation of all the wisdom and experience that went into your coding. It is an advertisement of your skills and ability that all the world can see. A little extra time and attention here can make a big difference in how you are perceived as a programmer.

There is one more consideration in function naming: the level or layer at which the function resides. Whatever convention you use to indicate the level, be sure that every exported function contains some reference to its home level. You do not have to use names that indicate levels at all; the name of a level can relate to its functionality. One of my favorite layer names was from a project I was on a few years ago; it was called kglue (pronounced "kay-glue"). The *k* stood for *kernel,* and the *glue* part referred to the fact that it was the place everyone had to go to get at any data in the kernel. It was a corny name, perhaps, but the fact that it was an elegant and supremely useful library is also part of the reason I'm so fond of it.

Tip: Name the levels of your architecture.

Names like high and low usually aren't adequate. Make them informative. Depending on the kind of software, you can use names such as user interface, engine, kernel, file utils, screen display, and so on. Use your imagination. Part of the trick of making C a real language is to invent interesting words and concepts. A mind is a terrible thing to waste.

2

In-Line Documentation

I'm not a fan of extensive in-line documentation. Sometimes, of course, it is the only way to document something. In some cases you have spent a great deal of time constructing code that is unreadable by anyone who can't invest the same amount of time you took. Perhaps you've written a macro that has more pointers than a bird-dog breeder. Perhaps you've got a pointer to a function that takes pointers to pointers to functions that take pointers to functions as arguments as its arguments. See what I mean? Some constructions are simply too compact to be easily readable, and there are good reasons for such things. In-line code was invented for such situations, although this kind of thing usually occurs inside a library, not in the exported stuff.

Most of the time, an excess of in-line documentation means that the programmer either has too much time on his hands or didn't really understand what he was coding. I would prefer that a programmer take the time to understand what he is working on, create useful names for things, and make the code speak for itself as much as possible. Clear, concise, readable code is also safer code.

Don't confuse in-line documentation with pseudocode, by the way. If you use pseudocode to block out the program, don't leave it there afterwards. The things you learned while writing and developing the actual code need to be reflected in any in-line documentation you elect to include.

If you do use in-line documentation, make it interesting. No one but the other programmers will ever see it, so let your imagination run free.

> *Tip:* Internal documentation is a wonderful opportunity to exercise creativity. Don't waste it!

Names as Documentation

This is the lowest level of documentation and, in my opinion, the most critical. It is useful, of course, to have good documentation at the higher levels. It is this sort of documentation, in fact, that

2

the other programmers who will use the tools you build rely on. But because it costs a company more to maintain code than to write it in the first place, names ultimately have more influence on how your code is used than any other form of documentation.

Warning: This section relies heavily on opinion, and opinions differ. Use with discretion!

The ideal variable name looks like this:

```
<prefix><descriptive name>
```

For example:

```
egFileHandle
```

In this example, the prefix is used to designate the level (engine), and the name itself includes the type of the variable (handle). There are as many ways to include this kind of information as there are programmers. You could just as easily name your variable like this:

```
ehFile
```

In this case, the prefix tells you two things: that the variable is used in the engine level (e) and that it is a handle (h).

> *Tip: How you standardize creating names is not nearly as important as the fact of standardization.*

In other words, what matters is not the convention, but that it be obvious and useful.

A large number of conventions are out there—all lowercase or mixed case, and all with different ideas about what a prefix or suffix is for. Some are good, some are atrocious, and most are reasonably useful. Perhaps someday there will be a single standard we can all rally around. Until then, at least you and your fellow programmers on a certain project should rally around no more than one standard for naming.

So much for the technical aspects.

2

Everything else about naming is subtle, personal, and hard to define. If you can get into the right frame of mind, however, you stand a much better chance of creating names that will mean something to the next person down the line. Or even to you after you've spent six weeks on a special project and you find yourself facing your own code again.

Naturally, that frame of mind involves our old friend, the programmer over your shoulder (the POYS for short). Evaluate your names from the point of view of the POYS. After all, he is ignorant of a lot of the day-to-day things you face, and he can't use them to interpret the names you create.

Some general rules about names can be stated. Engrave them on your frontal lobes:

◆ *Short names are better than long names.* No one wants to type out long names unnecessarily. However, you will notice that almost every other rule listed here tends to create longer, rather than shorter, names. This is a known problem, and it is the reason good naming is an art, not a science. In practice, I find that I tend to create rather long names, which I eventually whittle down to a manageable size after a little thought and experimentation. That's not a bad technique, from a practical point of view. Before you "publish" your names for others to use, ask yourself: Does the programmer over your shoulder think this name is too short, just right, or too long?

   Corollary: *Use shorter names for more frequently used functions. Don't waste them on little-used backwater stuff.*

◆ *Never use a short name if it is ambiguous or incomplete.* Don't shorten a name to the point where it is no longer clear what the name refers to. Don't leave out necessary terms.

◆ *Take the long view.* Other programmers will have to use this name, either right now because it's a tool you built for them, or later when they (or you) have to maintain this stretch of code. Be considerate of their needs. The long

2

view also refers to the breadth of the project. You might need to avoid stepping on the naming needs of other programmers, so adequately differentiate your names from others' names. Maybe the prefix isn't enough; maybe you need to repeat a certain word in a group of related functions to make sure it is clear that they are related to each other. Again, this tends to make names rather long. Weigh the cost and the benefits.

◆ *Use words.* I know this rule sounds obvious, but we've all seen names that look like the phonetic spelling of Middle Martian. Don't show off your early training in Greek. Don't try to crowd the largest possible number of consonants together. Do use whole words to make your point.

◆ *Don't abbreviate unless the abbreviated word is commonly used in a variety of names in the project.* The easiest—and most dangerous—way to shorten a name is to use abbreviations for the words you just used. If you abbreviate at will, you will find that the programmer over your shoulder gets confused. What is obvious to you is not obvious to others, so limit abbreviations to words that occur frequently in the names. If you are using exception handling to process errors, *ex* is an easy abbreviation to remember. It saves a lot of letters, and everyone can handle it. On the other hand, abbreviating *window* as *wd* when you hardly ever use windows would confuse just about everyone.

◆ *Follow prefix construction rules as though your life depended on it.* This is a constitutional issue. It is not negotiable. You should expect a jail sentence if you break this rule. A nation (and a project) lives well only if its citizens subscribe to certain unspoken common values. Freedom of the press, freedom of religion, and the right to bear arms (well, OK, that one gets debated) are the equivalent of agreeing on what prefixes to use in what situations. If these things are allowed to fall into disarray, civilization itself could follow. Enough said.

2

◆ *Don't use prefixes where they don't make sense.* For example, if you are iterating a variable i in a loop, prefixes would be silly.

Examples of Good Naming Conventions

Three examples are included here. They are not perfect, and not everyone will agree that they are even good, but I believe that these examples illustrate at least the most important things about good naming conventions.

Microsoft Windows

Hungarian notation aside, Windows does some things right. Windows functions are very wordy, of course, as are its constants. Maybe that's just because there are so darn many functions. Creating a useful naming convention gets harder as the number of functions rises. Even though Windows has its flaws, it does do a remarkable job of making it at least possible to program with such a large, complex API.

Look at some of the obvious naming successes from the Windows API. Consider the use of the word Get in the following function names:

```
Declare Function GetVersion Lib "Kernel" () As Integer
Declare Function GetNumTasks Lib "Kernel" () As Integer
Declare Function GetModuleHandle Lib "Kernel"
  (ByVal lpModuleName As String) As Integer
Declare Function GetModuleUsage Lib "Kernel"
  (ByVal hModule As Integer) As Integer
Declare Function GetModuleFileName Lib "Kernel"
  (ByVal hModule As Integer, ByVal lpFilename As String,
  ByVal nSize As Integer) As Integer
Declare Function GetInstanceData Lib "Kernel"
  (ByVal hInstance As Integer, ByVal pData As Integer,
  ByVal nCount As Integer) As Integer
```

Repetition is the soul of a good naming convention, and that is where the Windows API succeeds. Not only is Get repeated often,

2

but it is used in the same sense almost all the time. That is a recipe for effectiveness.

Although brevity is the soul of wit (and usually of a good naming convention), the sheer number of functions used in the API is mind-numbing, and you run out of good short names. (Of course, it almost seems that Windows entirely avoids short names, doesn't it? I can't think of many short names, good or otherwise.) Just cruising through the API, I came across this gem of a name:

```
Declare Sub SwitchStackBack Lib "Kernel" ()
```

Could be the name of a hit tune, maybe a hard-driving blues number: "Switch Stack Back, Jack!"

All joking aside, the Windows function names are long because Windows uses a different approach than a conventional API. Windows function names include verbs (like *get*, for example). This means that a function name is more like a sentence than a simple name, and that extra syntax drives up the letter count. The SwitchStackBack function is a prime example of this technique. Even though it's hard to type that sequence of ch/ck/ck without error, it's hard to forget the actual name.

C String Functions

The C string functions are probably the most frequently used functions in all of C. They are the first functions you meet when you start to learn how to program in C, and that is unfortunate. Meeting them that way makes them too much like integral parts of the language, rather than examples of what functions can be like.

The string functions are at the opposite end of the naming spectrum from the Windows API. These guys are short to the point of insult, as shown in Table 2.1.

Table 2.1. C standard library sample names.

Function	Abbreviations	Explanation
strcmp	str	Is a string function
	cmp	Compares strings
strcmpi	str	Is a string function
	cmp	Compares strings
	i	Is case-insensitive
strnicmp	str	Is a string function
	n	Compares a specified number of characters
	i	Is case-insensitive
	cmp	Compares strings
strstr	str	Is a string function
	str	Finds a string in a string

This makes me wonder—whatever happened to strstri? If SwitchStackBack were a blues number, I'd have to say that "strstr-i" would have to be a polka.

There are many other string functions, of course, but they all follow the same rules: short is sweet; shorter is sweeter. For functions that are used frequently, this approach works.

Platform-Specific Functions

Now look at a set of relatively compact functions: platform-specific functions in C. These are function names that have two parts: the usual function part (what the function does) and the operating-system designation. On a PC platform, two prefixes are commonly used: dos and bios (see Table 2.2).

2

Table 2.2. Sample platform-specific names.

Function	Abbreviations	Explanation
_dos_gettime	_dos_	This function relates specifically to MS-DOS.
	get	This function will definitely have a return value.
	time	This function returns the system time.
_dos_getftime	_dos_	This function relates specifically to MS-DOS.
	get	This function will definitely have a return value.
	f	This time relates to files, not to the system.
	time	This function returns the time the file was last written to.
_bios_keybrd	_bios_	This function makes a call into the PC BIOS.
	keybrd	This function deals with the keyboard-related BIOS functions.
_bios_printer	_bios_	This function makes a call into the PC BIOS.
	printer	This function initializes the printer.

Note that these function names are longer than those for the string functions. Because they are platform-specific, they have a smaller audience and thus can be longer. Note also the leading underscore: it is often used by compiler vendors to indicate non-ANSI-compatible functions.

2

I think it is smart to pay some kind of penalty for using platform-specific functions. The preceding underscore, the spelling out of the operating system name and the word "bios"—all of these help these functions stand out in your code. It is advantageous to be able to keep track of platform-dependent code, and I like to think that that is the very reason for the style of this particular naming convention.

There are many other good examples of library naming conventions. A certain company might put its initials in front of its library functions, either to distinguish themselves from the competition or to warn you away, depending on the quality of the library.

The permutations on naming are endless, so remember these basic rules:

Rule 1: The fact of standardization is more important than the method.

Rule 2: Stick to obvious conventions and consistent *abbreviations.*

Rule 3: Small libraries use small names; big libraries use sentences for names.

3

Writing Code

3

So far I've been talking about programming from a pretty abstract perspective. Now it's time to look at the nitty-gritty, day-in, day-out stuff of programming.

How do you write code? Do you sit down at a terminal and write it out? Or do you reflect a bit beforehand, and code only when you have thought it through? Have you ever broken your habits into steps and asked yourself whether they work for you or against you? Most of us don't have the time or the inclination for much introspection.

There are no hard and fast rules about writing effective code. Some of us work best sitting down and writing a little code to see how it works, and others like to think about it beforehand. There are many other approaches as well.

See where you fit into the following programmer personalities:

◆ The Perfectionist seems to take forever to get out a piece of working code. Subspecies include Redesigners, Renamers, Structuralists, Parametizers, and Nitpickers.

◆ The Slob thinks that coding is like Italian food: anything can be covered with a palatable sauce. Subspecies include Spaghetti (every line of code is related to every other line of code), Lasagna (Readable code? Say what?), and Rotelli ("It goes round and round and comes out somewhere").

◆ The Genius has two important subspecies: the ones who actually are geniuses, and the ones who think they are geniuses. It is very important to distinguish between them, but it is not always easy.

◆ The Workhorse is willing to stay up all night just to get the calling conventions right. He met his programming muse when he was three years old. Subspecies include Mules ("I don't care if it works; I just want to write code"), Gamers ("I'll get to it this afternoon; I've got this little thing I'm writing right now"), and Monomaniacs ("I know it's harder this way. So?").

◆ The Debugger is born to debug, because he can't write three lines of code without a bug. He is best used in test and maintenance, because he knows all the ways that things can go wrong (from personal experience). There are no important subspecies.

◆ The Purist dreams in C code (and very elegant code at that). He wishes he could carry on a casual conversation in C. The two significant subspecies are the ones who understand English as well as C, and the ones who don't.

◆ The Kid, sometimes known as the Star, is not just a genius, but he's also a showman, a ringleader, and a motivator. Other programmers rally around his ideas, good or bad. A future Architect.

◆ The Architect is a great conceptualizer. He can include more ideas in a sentence than most of us could put in a book. Subspecies include Arrogant and Humble (rare; sightings disputed, range unknown). Omnivorous.

All humor aside, programming is a challenging job. I've met very few programmers who didn't give some thought to what they would do "after programming." It is stressful, it is often thankless, and (particularly in some parts of the country) it is not always financially rewarding. There are two ways to respond to these issues:

◆ Increase job satisfaction by writing code of which you can be proud.

◆ Help each other by writing code that won't drive the next programmer nuts.

You will notice a common thread there, and throughout this book:

Rule: There is no substitute for good programming style.

3

Version and Change Control

Formal version control forms the Great Divide in programming today. On one side are all the projects that do it informally, and on the other side are those with formal version and change control. It's a lot like the situation in the Old West, with the free-range cattlemen on one side and the farmers (and their fences) on the other.

There's a lot to be said for free-range programming. The individual programmer has a lot more say in what's going on, and more freedom to implement as he sees fit. There aren't a whole lot of forms to fill out, and changes aren't such a big deal that someone feels compelled to hold a meeting to discuss every one of them. On the other hand, if a change doesn't work, it might take a week to get back to where you started.

There's a lot to be said for version and change control. A mistake can be pulled back out of the code automatically. The boss can answer (most of) his boss' questions.

The big question, though, is this: Is the time you save by controlling these things worth the effort and the loss of individual space? Yes and no. (What did you expect?)

Like everything else in the universe, this is a question of balance. A control system that gives programmers the feeling that they are working on an assembly line is a problem. A system that makes programmers feel that they have no idea where the next attack is coming from is also a problem.

The need for controls is not as related to the size of a project as you might expect. I recall a rather major project (more than 30 programmers) that had used a manual system for integrating changes into the baseline code. Someone decided to add tighter controls to the process, so every change had to be independently tested to see whether it caused problems.

3

This testing step (not to be confused with the Test Division, which continued to do the same things it had always done) wound up involving (among other things) the following:

◆ Sixty PCs, with associated hard drives, monitors, cabling, automatic switchers, driver software, and so on

◆ An upgrade to a UNIX host so that it could monitor the 60 PCs without overloading I/O capabilities

◆ Writing software for the host to control the 60 PCs

◆ Writing and revising tens of thousands of test suites to interface with the automatic system

◆ Making all test suites conform to one input, output, and reporting standard

◆ Hiring almost a dozen people to program, maintain, and service the new system

This was, needless to say, overkill. This expenditure of time, people, and money produced these results:

◆ The programmers stopped testing their own code, so the new people began receiving code that would not compile.

◆ The people manning the new step were completely unfamiliar with the programmers and how they worked, resulting in a near-total lack of effective communication when problems needed to be solved.

◆ So much energy went into revising tests that no one stopped to ask whether the tests were any good in the first place.

Control, in and of itself, is not necessarily a good thing. It is a tool, and like any tool it can be used well, ineffectively, or as a weapon.

A little control is a good thing. It's like the muzzle on a trained bear: under all reasonable circumstances, it's not even necessary. But when things get weird, it is essential.

3

Tip: Add controls only to guarantee that chaos will not reign. A little chaos is not only tolerable but beneficial.

No project can work without some cracks in the system, the little places where programming miracles happen, the places where ideas are born. And no project can work without some degree of control, either.

Write for Your Audience

This is the one section of the book that is entirely about the programmer over your shoulder (POYS). I'll let Clarence, the programmer over *my* shoulder, have his say.

"Being the POYS can be very frustrating. The things I've seen! I'm tempted to just list all the horrors I've witnessed and beg you never to do such things, but I know from experience that you won't listen to that, because it's just too darn depressing. So I'll try to stick to the positive stuff.

"There isn't a piece of code written that shouldn't eventually be read by someone else. You have quite an audience if you think about it:

"The weekly code walk-through. What? You don't have weekly code walk-throughs? Don't you realize how critical other viewpoints are? You are not the first to encounter these problems. You can learn a lot from programmers who have been here before, and you also can learn a lot from programmers who aren't as involved as you are. They can see the forest, not the trees whose lower branches you keep bumping into.

"Anyone who has to debug your code. Did you know that the guy in testing knows enough about C that he checks the source code when he finds a bug? Did you know that he gives up on some programmers because their code is so unclear?

"You, when you have to fix that bug six months later. How long will it take you to reinvent what you did the first time so that you can fix the bug?

"The maintenance people, the folks who will inherit what you have written a year or more down the road.

"So forgive me if I seem to have an attitude."

Code as Text: Being a Good Author

I have been trying to make a case for C as a true language. If you are using C just to make things happen in a machine, it's hard to get it to work like a language.

Writing intelligent C has much in common with writing a good novel. The required skills for each are listed in the following table:

What Makes a Good Novel	Corresponding C Skills
Strong characterization	Well-written tools that show up in a variety of scenes (oops—I mean modules!).
Excitement and adventure	You've got to be kidding!
Plot	Specification.
Suspense	Will Anthony ever get the virtual memory scheme working? Is it possible to speed up the screen I/O?
Clear writing	Naming conventions; imbedding clear concepts in object names, structures, macros, and so on.
A sound main idea	Is there an overall plan or design?

3

Code as Code: Stop, Look, and Listen

As much as I have harped about C as a real language, there is an inevitable level at which it is simply code. The rule here is simple:

Rule: Never forget that one member of your audience is a machine—a completely unforgiving, idiotic machine.

No matter how far you reach for elegance, you must never allow your feet to leave the ground. There is a word for such flights of fancy: bugs. They breed in the rarefied air of "I already know how to do this; let's fancy it up (the old "just one more feature" won't hurt" approach)."

Do you know assembly language for the platform you work on? Despite the wide variety of platforms on which C can be found, it remains intimately tied to assembly-language concepts. It is well worth your time to debug in mixed-language mode if that is available to you. (Of course, you must turn off optimization for this to be meaningful.) Even if you do not have formal experience with assembly language, you will see pretty quickly how C code breaks down to the next lower level.

Optimization and Obfuscation

Optimization involves a necessary trade-off in clarity. To optimize means to make something closer to the machine, to move human readability in favor of machine readability. There will always be a need to optimize, and there will always be a penalty for it. The key is to minimize the penalty.

Tip: If code can be tweaked, so can comments.

If you are going to take shortcuts, if you are going to do some whiz-bang, fancy, guts-of-the-machine programming, for pity's sake leave a trail of bread crumbs for the next person down the line.

3

You are certain to have some insights as you comb through the various iterations of the code that are critical to understanding what you have done. Share those thoughts! The best coders I know aren't afraid to wax philosophical at times to explain (don't think in terms of justifying, please!) what they have done, and why.

If you can express your ideas in clear English, you will inevitably do a better job of expressing them in code, too.

There's Nowhere to *goto*

The bane of C is the goto statement. For a language with so few actual statements, would it have been so bad to leave this one out?

Fact of life: I have yet to see C code using goto statements that was worth the time it took to figure it out.

Most often, using a goto is just another way of saying, "I didn't think this through. Now I'm stuck and I refuse to start over, so I'm going to use a goto statement."

Every once in a while, a situation is so complex that the price of a goto is less than the price of doing without it. Because a goto costs about what the Hope diamond costs, this is a very, very rare occurrence. I recommend a good deal of thought before you give in and goto.

Tip: The road to ruin is lined with easy ways out.

4

C Testing

4

You could make a good case for the idea that programmers are not good testers. The usual reason cited is that they're just too close to their code to test it properly. There is a certain amount of truth to this.

When I managed a hardware/software testing laboratory, I found that the best testers were those who tried to bend the application in directions it was never intended to go. As a programmer works to make the program do certain (hopefully well-defined) things, he may have difficulty imagining the ways others will use that code or application.

This section of the book contains some ideas about how you can overcome the natural programmer's bias.

Test, Test, Test

Rule: Testing is an integral part of the programming process.

I know this seems obvious, but it is not obvious in practice. The demands on a programmer's time almost always stress actual *programming* time. Sometimes it seems as though everyone wants a perfect piece of code, but no one has allowed any time for testing it. Those are the bad days.

It appears that there is one fundamental fact about programming that eludes notice all too frequently:

Fact: Programming is an iterative process.

Again, this is obvious. It's obvious because we all know that every program has mistakes in it just waiting for the next opportunity to show up. But if it is so obvious, why is this fact ignored so often? At best, some token "fudge factor" will be slotted into the schedule for dealing with unexpected faults. This has to do with human nature. We all have a built-in safety valve—it's hard to see our own mistakes.

Testing Is an Attitude

The best testing happens when the tester has an attitude about the test object. By "attitude" I'm referring to the slang meaning, as in "What's with him? He's got a real attitude."

Testing is the moral equivalent of war—and a dirty war at that. The key strategy in testing is the search-and-destroy mission. In and of itself, testing is boring: repeated key stroking, record keeping, the insane need for repeatability—all of these things demand patience and a love for detail. Alone, however, such testing is not enough to get the job done. That's where the search-and-destroy mission comes in.

To begin a successful testing session, you must first adopt the mind-set of a hungry, ticked-off Marine. First of all, you are in enemy territory—you are now the user, and you are faced with a black box whose continued proper operation threatens your livelihood (if you can't break it, you're not doing your job).

So don't just sit in your foxhole looking for suspicious movement in your vicinity. Like the true hunter that you are, you need to move through enemy territory looking for bugs. Don't be nice about it—go where you don't have any right to go, try things no one in his right mind would ever do. Face it: that's what's really going on out there, isn't it? That's how you find bugs, faults, anomalies, or whatever else you choose to call them.

My best tester was a woman who would come in each morning with a cheerful but determined look on her face. She would get her morning coffee, sit down at her terminal, and set out to find bugs—and she always found them. Although she wasn't the brightest tester and didn't have the most experience, her attitude gave her an advantage. When she found a bug, it was always a good one, and she would often storm into my office, slam the bug report down on my desk, and get this big smirk on her face. She knew that some programmer, somewhere, had been beaten. You've got to love someone who can compete like that, even if it's your code she just trashed. The trick, of course, is to treat your own code like that.

4

Who Tests Your Code? You Do!

Fact: A programmer who doesn't test his own code is looking for trouble.

I have seen programmers deliver code that wouldn't even compile. I also have seen programmers who routinely sifted every morsel of code through a rigorous testing regime. Presuming that you are now convinced you should test your code, how do you go about it? Start with one important fact:

Fact: You can never test every line of code.

This is a simple mathematical reality. Think of all the `fish`, switches, loops, and other flow-control statements in your code. Even a relatively small program has a sufficient variety of inputs, flow-controls, and outputs to make it impossible to test more than a fraction of the code. For a large, commercial application, it's even worse.

Some compilers come with code profilers, which do provide some assistance in analyzing what is going on in the code. There are also some sophisticated (and thus expensive) programs available that can help you determine how good your test coverage is. It is a simple mathematical reality, however, that the flow of control through the code is far too complex to ever test it completely.

Given that even the very best testing is a hit-and-miss proposition, the trick is to test where you are most likely to find problems. The question is, Where are you most likely to find problems? That's easy: wherever you are least likely to look for them. There are some basic approaches you can use to establish a useful testing system:

Rule: No change is too small to require testing.

If you make even a tiny change to your code, test it. Almost anything you add, subtract, or change in your code has effects elsewhere. Did you leave out a parameter? Did you misuse a macro? Did you use a local when you should have used a global? Did you forget to delete the old line of code? Need I say more?

Rule: Test for valid inputs.

The most embarrassing thing that can happen to a programmer is to have someone input obviously correct data only to get an obviously incorrect result. If there are known, valid inputs, define at least one representative input for each correct type of input. For example, if a screen can be used to input only numeric data, make sure you have at least one of each kind of numeric data: positive integer, negative integer, zero, one, and positive and negative real numbers (for those of you who don't remember college math, these include numbers with decimal points).

Corollary: Test the extremes and the boundaries of valid inputs.

Don't forget those obvious special cases in which the data is correct but in an unusual format (for example `0001`, `1.0000000000000000000000000`, `237.`, or `0000000`).

For any valid input, there are usually two extremes: the smallest and the largest. *Small* extends to many things, including the smallest value, the smallest number of digits or characters, and so on. Similarly, *large* can mean many things. It can mean putting $12 billion in a numeric entry, or it can mean putting only zeroes in an entry that allows up to 14 digits.

Rule: Test for invalid inputs.

This test is harder. You can usually define all cases of valid input, but knowing when you have gotten every case of invalid input is like knowing when to stop eating potato chips. Again, "attitude" is useful in coming up with invalid data. Think to yourself, "How can I break this? What would really mess it up? Does the program take numbers?" Naturally, you'll want to enter some letters, just to see what happens. Does it take dollar amounts? What happens when the user enters commas and dollar signs? What if the user puts in more than one decimal point? Inputs that answer those questions in the affirmative are excellent test candidates.

4

Corollary: Test the boundaries of invalid inputs.

Does the field take 10 characters? If so, try 11. Make sure things stop where they are supposed to stop. This kind of testing is known as "boundary testing" because it defines the limits of performance and acceptable data entry. In fact, it defines all aspects of the program.

Rule: Test for small, concrete things.

How do you tell whether the test was a success or a failure? You have to limit yourself to tests that produce a verifiable result. Sometimes this means breaking something down into ridiculously tiny pieces so that each piece can be verified. You run a test only to generate data, and that data is useless unless you can evaluate it effectively.

Corollary: Every test has a single, defined, predicted result.

Of course, there will be those times when the predicted result is not the correct result, so watch out!

Rule: Half of your test effort should involve logically derived tests.

These are the kinds of tests that you, the programmer, can write better than anyone else. You know what is going on in the code, and you can write tests that will attack the code where it is weakest or most complex. You are the only one who can know which sections of the code deserve the most attention.

Rule: Half of your test effort should involve things no one in his right mind would do.

What's crazy for one person is perfectly sane for the next person ("You say to-may-toe, I say to-mah-toe"). That's just how it is (refer to the previous section on search-and-destroy missions).

Rule: Keep good records.

If you have designed good tests, the results should be in a form that can be stored for later review. Consider the following scenario: A bug is found by someone running the tests you designed for your code. It takes the person a week to get back to you, and

4

you say to yourself, "Hey, I ran that same test and the code was fine!" So you look through your records, and there it is. The test passed when you ran it. It looks as though the problem cropped up only when your code was merged into the baseline. The problem might be yours—and it might not. At least you know it's not a problem internal to your code; it might be somewhere else, somewhere down the line.

Rule: Look for trends.

Which modules generate the most test failures? Which are the most robust? Which modules require the greatest and the least number of changes? What kinds of errors do you tend to make? What tests could you devise that would help you catch these kinds of errors?

Rule: Walk through your code, pretending you are the CPU.

The simplest test is to pretend that you are the CPU. You're not as fast and your arithmetic unit has some flaws, but your cerebrum has some capabilities that go well beyond the best CPU—things like the ability to

◆ Notice when a line of code is repeated twice.

◆ See where the code is not as efficient as it needs to be.

◆ See where the code is confusing and ambiguous.

◆ See where the logic breaks from the design.

Rule: Keep your attitude sour, belligerent, and nasty—don't give yourself even the slightest benefit of the doubt.

Be hard on yourself. Write tests that push your code to the limit and beyond. Remember: if you don't find those inevitable bugs, someone else will. Wouldn't it be nice if you could hand the code to the programmer over your shoulder? ("Here, Clarence, take a look at this for me, will you? I'll be at the water cooler if you need me.")

5

Modular Testing

5

Modular testing is a lot like modular programming. In its simplest form, they are identical—you write tests for each module you are working on—but modular testing can also be more subtle than that. You do not have to establish a one-to-one correspondence between program modules and test modules. What you need is a test plan.

> *Tip: Testing without a plan is like flying without an airplane—it's over quickly, and the results are less than satisfactory.*

Developing a good test plan is not the easiest thing in the world to do; it requires the ability to see into the future. The test plan must anticipate both planned design elements and exigencies of change over time. Nonetheless, your intrepid servant is willing to lay down a few rules that should help you get a grip on your test plan:

> *Rule: Assume your own ignorance.*

You can never anticipate everything, but this is especially true in testing. Because you're building the tests on top of a design that cannot anticipate everything, you'll be anticipating even less.

> *Rule: Ask yourself how you will test it.*

There are many ways to run a test: people can sit at a bunch of terminals and pound away; a master program can control slave programs running multiple iterations of automated tests; people at terminals can execute scripts; a control program can execute the code and monitor results, all on one computer or in one session; and so on.

The test method affects the test plan in several ways:

◆ Manual testing involves less coverage, but the fact that an actual human being is doing it means that unexpected avenues may be discovered.

◆ Automated testing lends itself to good record keeping of the test results. This is very useful for tracking regressions (things that break after being fixed).

◆ Automated testing always walks down the same path. This predictability, however, is a handicap when you have new code to test, or if some part of the code isn't covered by the automated tests.

The critical issues in developing a test plan are coverage, method, resources, and reporting.

Test Coverage

As mentioned previously, it is impossible to write enough tests to cover every line of code. As a programmer, you are in a somewhat better position than the folks over in the test department. They have to treat the application like a "black box"—they never know if they've actually covered the right code with the right tests. So, coverage is a matter of addressing the most important sections of the code.

What are the most important sections of the code? Well, how about anyplace where the most bugs show up? That's accurate, but not very helpful.

There are a number of approaches to this problem, but I prefer a very simple and human one. It's based on this rule:

Rule: Complicated code generates more bugs than simple code—focus your efforts there.

This is not a criticism. Often, code gets complicated because the job it has to do is, well, complicated. The good thing about this rule is that it is a useful guide for a programmer when it comes time to write some tests.

As a programmer, you can do what is called "white-box" testing—the exact opposite of black-box testing. You know what is in the code, so use that information to design your tests.

Some candidates for the designation "complicated code" are the following:

◆ *Lots of indirection.* Unless you are a master of indirection, this can cause problems.

5

◆ *Lots of control structures.* For example, nesting and long switch statements are worth serious attention.

◆ *Recursion.* It's a useful code saver, but also a good bug generator if you make a mistake.

◆ *Functions with many parameters.* The more parameters, the more possibilities for mistakes.

◆ *New code.* First-time code tends to be less well organized than mature code, so test it well.

There are other kinds of code that lend themselves to testing, but in a different way.

Rule: *To find bugs, go where the data are.*

As a datum moves around in the program, it passes from one section of code to another until, somewhere, something wrong happens and the datum gets mangled. There are sections of code that are "data bottlenecks." These are the sections that process more than their share of data. If you focus testing in such an area, you may not catch a bug in action, but you might see the effects of one: bad data. You will have to trace back to see what caused the bug, but the hard part is over—you know there's a bug.

Rule: *You can't predict everything, so don't try.*

Ultimately, you cannot get the kind of test coverage you want. It's a mistake to assume that focusing on key areas will find all the bugs. There will also be some bugs where there shouldn't be—in the simple, straightforward parts of the code. Elegant code creates elegant bugs, not freedom from bugs. Spend some time testing the sections of your code where you would least expect a problem, just in case.

Testing Methods

I've already hinted at the major possibilities, but I'll reiterate:

◆ Human, free-form testing

◆ Human, scripted testing

5

- ◆ Self-automated testing

- ◆ Automated testing

Human testing has the advantage of having a (more or less) independent-thinking organism doing the testing. Unusual and unexpected phenomena are often noticed and followed up. Free-form testing is best left to folks who are naturally good testers—that is, people who have no qualms about savaging a programmer's efforts.

The disadvantage of human testing is that it is expensive. It takes time to sit there and press those keys or click that mouse. It is an expensive, but necessary, way (usually) to test software.

Automated testing, on the other hand, can be economical (if you ignore the legion of test writers required to feed the beast). Once a test is written, it can be run over and over and over again. The software itself can execute the test (if it's that kind of software), or a control program can execute the test. The control program can be either local, in which case it is part of the current session and can mask certain kinds of errors, or remote, in which case it has little or no impact on the session being tested.

There are many ways to run both human and automated testing sessions. Repeatability, of course, is very, very important. For free-form testing, some method for recording all events is essential. There's nothing worse than realizing that the horrible bug you just encountered was caused by a keystroke sequence you can't recall (maybe it was caused by the menu you invoked but never used, for example).

Repeatability is not a problem for automated testing. Automated tests, however, may be too simple to discover certain kinds of bugs. Automated tests simply lack the killer instinct of a good human tester. Ultimately, each kind has its place in the test plan.

Testing Resources

How long does it take to test code? At least as long as it took to write it in the first place.

5

Rule: It takes as long to test as it does to code.

Does this surprise you? If it does, ask yourself this question and answer it honestly: Do other people find most of the bugs in your code? If they do, you are not testing your code adequately. You need to step back and look at it from another perspective. You probably need simply to spend more time on testing.

Whether you are a one-man operation or part of a larger project or organization, testing may feel like something that cuts into your programming time. You're wrong. Testing time *is* programming time.

Programming is an iterative process. The essence of an iterative process is the following:

◆ Do something.

◆ Get feedback.

◆ Do it again, only better.

Substituting some programming concepts for generic ones produces the following:

◆ Write code.

◆ Run tests and evaluate results.

◆ Fix bugs and correct design errors.

I will admit that this model does not work for every programmer. There are programmers who are better than others at writing code, and there are programmers who can easily fix and correct problems. It's worth a little digression to see what this means for programming.

Some programmers tend to write code with only a few bugs. These programmers are usually the ones who try to get it right the first time, the ones who try to avoid spending any time at all in the feedback part of the loop. Typically, these programmers produce less code each day, but they spend less time on iterations, so, in theory, the time factor should even out.

Other programmers tend to write code with a greater number of bugs. Typically, they're not concerned with getting it right the first time; they're concerned with getting it right eventually. They use the feedback part of the cycle (debugging) to get information about the coding process. These programmers write more code each day, but they spend more time on iterations, so, again in theory, the time factor should even out.

Usually, it does even out, except for the wizards at one end of the spectrum (those who can get it right the first time with consistency), and the Sluggo's at the other end of the spectrum (those who produce one or more bugs for every one they fix).

> **Rule:** *Whatever method you choose (you didn't know it was a choice, did you?), you have a responsibility to deliver good code.*

This rule is comforting because *delivering* good code is a lot easier than *writing* good code. ("As if Hemingway ever got it right the first time," Clarence says.) Keep this distinction in mind the next time you feel challenged at your terminal.

> **Corollary:** *Given enough time, even a monkey can write a solid binary search algorithm.*

Thus, there is no excuse for not finding the resources to test adequately. Unless you have test results that give you a good feeling in the pit of your stomach about the code, it's not ready for prime time. That's worth repeating:

> **Rule:** *Unless you have test results that give you a good feeling in the pit of your stomach about the code, it's not ready for release.*

If you can't test it, don't write it.

Test Reporting

Say what? I'll bet you never even gave this a thought.

Maybe test reporting is a little too esoteric for programmer consideration, and maybe not. Test reporting is primarily an issue

5

on large development projects. When there is an independent team generating test results, you need a way to get the test results to the programmers.

What does a test result look like? Well, it looks like lots of things:

◆ It looks like a screen dump that has the wrong colors on line 16, positions 17 through 25.

◆ It looks like a report that has transposed columns.

◆ It looks like a report with incorrect data.

◆ It looks like the machine hung when the test was run, and there are no results.

◆ It looks like the test itself is in error and the code is fine.

◆ It looks like there might or might not be an error.

It can be frustrating to see a test fail, knowing it's going to take hours just to find out what, in fact, went wrong. If the test was not written with the idea that the results must be meaningful, trouble results.

Sometimes a bug occurs in the "overhead" section of a test—the part of the test code dedicated to setup, communication, or reporting triggers an error. When that happens, three things can happen: the error is included in the test report; the error is not included in the test report because the test failed to finish; or the error makes no difference to the test report. In the latter case, you won't even know that the test failed. Be aware of these possibilities. Test failures can be quite obscure.

The worst case, of course, is when the test itself is wrong, and the error it reports is a false error. These are called *test artifacts*, and they can be a real hassle to uncover. If someone else writes the test that reports the false error, it's even harder. Ideally, each test reports one thing. For convenience, you can group tests into suites, with each test suite covering no more than a module (white-box testing) or a functional area (black-box testing). Test reports for an entire suite are easily summarized for convenience.

5

Back to Basics: What Is a Module?

Now that you know more than you ever hoped to about testing, let's back up a bit and consider the subject of testing your own modules. From a testing standpoint, what is a module?

I have a rule for C-language code that goes like this:

Rule: *For testing purposes, a module starts with a top-level left curly brace ({), and ends with the matching right curly brace (}).*

In other words, if you have a file with seven related functions in it, you should strongly considering attacking it from seven different angles for testing purposes. Why? For the same reason you break code into modules: control.

The odds are against you the minute you try to test—you can't possibly cover all of the code, and you can't possibly write perfect tests. If you at least test the "lowest common denominator," you only have to think about one small, manageable thing at a time. (You do write small, manageable functions, right?)

The Principles of Module Testing

Depending on the nature of the code, there are only a few ways to get information into and out of the module. From a testing point of view, there are three ways to get the data into a function or module for testing:

Method 1: Do it by hand.

This is potentially tedious. I would recommend it only for the simplest modules and functions. You can do it with a code walk though (which is never a bad idea, even for more complex code, if you supplement it with other testing techniques) or you can do it by sitting down, making a copy of the module, adding a bit of code, compiling, running, and evaluating the results.

Method 2: Write a caller to make it up and stuff it in.

The next step up the evolutionary ladder is to leave your code alone and write something that will be the code you want to test. The caller can have hard-coded parameters, but that's not much better than Method 1. At least, write a caller with either input routines that you can use to stuff various (useful and well-thought-out) data into the code to be tested. If you are in the mood, you can have the caller generate random data. Be sure to include a routine in your caller that writes the results of each call somewhere where you can get a look at it later.

Method 3: Write a controller to stuff in what you tell it to.

A controller is the final step up the evolutionary ladder; it's the testing equivalent of mammals. A controller is a user-friendly version of the caller in Method 2. A controller has two important properties:

◆ The code in the controller is ironclad, bug proof to the nth degree.

◆ The controller is so simple to use that a monkey could get repeatable results.

I'll give you an example of one of the best controllers I ever encountered.

The project involved writing a compiler. At the core of the compiler was a parser that received certain expressions. If an expression was received under certain conditions, it was handled one way. Under other conditions, it was handled differently.

The conditions were expressed as a pattern of bits in a 16-bit datum. The original version of the controller had two critical flaws: there was no easy way to find out which bits had to be set for what conditions, and there was no easy way to translate from bits to bytes. (There never is, is there?)

The programmer who wrote the controller, however, didn't have those problems. He knew the decimal representation of every bit pattern that was actually used in the code, and he could use the controller easily and without error to test his code. No problem.

Later, when the testing division found out what a great tool he had developed, they had to put a little front end on it.

Here's the nicest part about this little item: the code for the tool was part of the module. To include the tool code in the object file, all you had to do was put a certain DEFINE on the command line when you ran the compiler. If you compiled one way, you had on object file to reference in the link file for the compiler. If you compiled the other way, you had a testing tool that was completely up to date! Now that's slick, and worth imitating.

Closing the Loopholes Is Easier than Finding Them

Fact: *It takes far more time and energy to find a bug than it does to correct it once it is found.*

This is true unless, of course, you manage to imbed a bug in every other line of code (in that case, once you find the first one, the rest are easy). No matter how long it takes you to fix a bug, a lot of resources went into finding it. Perhaps a bank of hundreds of test suites was run against the code for hours until the bug was finally smoked out. Perhaps the software went to the user and there's a lot of explaining to do. Either way, it cost a lot to find the bug. That's why it's so important for you, the programmer, to understand what it takes to put a test together for your own code.

6

Functional Testing

6

Functional testing is the testing done by other people, either the testing division (if you work for a big company) or the customer (if you have a small shop and ask your customer to do the testing). Although this kind of testing happens outside of your purview, it's worth knowing what's going on so you can use the process to your best advantage.

Functional testing is always "black-box" testing—the tester is deliberately ignorant about what's in the code and is concerned strictly with input and output. The weakness of this approach is that there is no way to concentrate on complex areas of code that might really need testing. That is why your testing—"white-box" testing—is so important.

The advantage of black-box testing is that you are blind to any assumptions made in the code. A complex piece of code, for example, may prove to be too slow, and it may need to be simplified or optimized. I think that it would be highly instructive for you, the programmer, to do some functional testing of someone else's code. This gives you a unique perspective on the programming process, and you learn that there are other programming issues than the ones you thought about before.

Tip: It's the little things that count.

When I ran a testing operation, I discovered that there are a lot of little things that programmers sometimes forget to think about (a kind of "can't see the forest for the trees" syndrome, if you will). For example, there were times when I received code that would not compile; sometimes I received firmware that contained old code (someone had forgotten to get the latest version of the code before making a change); other times software arrived that had the input turned off—convenient for the programmer who only wanted to test one thing, but not good for us.

Theoretically, functional testing is done to verify adherence to the design or the specification. In fact, you must often use it to discover things that should have been caught closer to home.

Why You Should Be an Active Participant

6

The primary purpose of functional testing is to verify whether the software does what it is supposed to do. Several things can get in the way of that:

◆ Unreported design changes. ("That's not a bug! We changed the design.")

◆ Unintended design changes. ("Hmm...it works better that way, doesn't it?")

◆ Bad design. ("It'll never fly if it works like that.")

Thus, ignore functional testing at your peril. Even on a moderately large project, some design changes are going to slip between the cracks. Sometimes these occur because of some misplaced paperwork or because someone gets a brilliant idea, puts it in the code, and never tells anyone. Such things tend to show up in the functional testing, and they can have wide-ranging effects. In many cases, the functional test is the only time these changes show up.

Sometimes, the project specification will be a little hazy about something. When that happens, there are two things programmers can do: talk it over with someone or make a decision. In practice, there's a lot more of the latter than the former. Most of the time, we're right, of course. Occasionally, we're more than right—we get a better idea than the designer and implement it that way. Often we don't even realize we've done it; it seems obvious.

The functional testers are going to come back to you telling you that you made a bug. Tell them, "Yes, it has wings like a bug, and it has eyes like a bug, but it also has feathers, so it's a bird and ought to be left alone to soar."

6

Changes in the Design Don't Have to Be Disasters

Module testing gives you immediate feedback about your code. Functional testing gives the designers semi-immediate feedback about the design. Once functional testing begins, there's a pretty good chance that the design changes will start in earnest because it is now obvious what works and what doesn't.

On some larger projects, there is a separate test effort called *usability testing*. This testing includes such things as testing the user interface with real users, assessing the logic of the key stroking, etc. For the purpose of discussion, I am including it with functional testing. As far as a programmer is concerned, these are really two of a kind.

> *Tip: Assume from the beginning that there will be design changes.*

The ways to cope with design changes are fairly mundane:

◆ *Write readable code.* When you go back to make the change, it's nice to know what you're working with.

◆ *Use tools.* It's easier to modify code built with bite-size tools than a mush built with whatever code was handy.

◆ *Use layers.* As often as not, the design changes can be handled in the higher layers, which are easier to modify than the whole lot of code at once.

This sounds like a synopsis of the rest of the book, doesn't it? Why do you think I've been exhorting you to do those things? Think of this book as Moe, your terminal or computer as Larry, and yourself (the programmer) as Curly (or Shep). If the book seems to whap you over the head occasionally, it's for your own good. Now eat your soup, and don't slurp.

6

Functional Testing as the Beginning of Code Maintenance

Functional testing is really the beginning of code maintenance for one simple reason: when the results of functional testing come back, you're going to be making changes to your code. If you have prepared well, it will be only moderately painful.

Rule: Maintenance starts closer to home than we realize.

We'll get into the details of code maintenance a little later. For now, the important thing to realize is this:

Fact: There is no getting away from it.

The moment you close your editor for the day—heck, the moment your mind wanders while writing code—you close the door on coding, and open the door on maintenance. Even if you hate everyone else around you and would love to befuddle them with sloppy code, don't do it to yourself.

7

C Debugging

7

Some programmers think that debugging is really maintenance, but not us, right? Debugging is an art. Unfortunately, the best debuggers are often the worst programmers and vice versa.

If testing requires an attitude, debugging requires one, too. The mindset required for good programming involves good conceptualizing. It also requires the ability to attend to details for very long stretches of time, and it doesn't hurt to work well with numbers and algorithms.

Debugging demands that you display the skills of both a physician and a detective. When you go to the doctor, you go with nothing more than a list of symptoms. It is up to the doctor to determine several things:

◆ Of those symptoms, which are irrelevant and which indicate some disease?

◆ What diseases have those symptoms?

◆ How should I treat the disease?

This translates into the kinds of things a programmer asks when debugging:

◆ Which of the errors and bugs at hand are relevant to the current problem, and which are not?

◆ What kinds of bugs tend to generate this kind of error? Is it a memory overwrite? Is it a protection fault? Or doesn't this operating system support a protected mode?

◆ Once the bug is identified, how can I fix it? Is it just a typo or does the code have to be rethought?

The detective also has some useful skills:

◆ The ability to uncover and closely examine available clues

◆ The stubbornness to pound the streets looking for additional clues

◆ The insight to apply the clues to the problem at hand and to ignore extraneous clues

A detective also frequently has a sidekick who does the dirty work. If you can manage that, good for you.

It should be obvious how to apply these skills to debugging:

♦ You will need to examine the code to find clues about the nature of the bug. The source of the bug may well be in someone else's code, for example, if you are using tools exported from someone else's library.

♦ Debugging can take a long time. I have spent days just tracking down a bug. It takes persistence to solve those kinds of bugs, especially when you are learning new things along the way and have to start all over because of it.

♦ Insight is not something that comes for free; it comes from exposing yourself to information. So, loosen your trench coat and expose yourself to new ideas as you debug.

At one time I lived in Portland, Oregon. In downtown Portland there is a semi-abstract bronze statue of a person with long, flowing hair. One day, someone put on a trench coat and stood before the statue, spreading open the trench coat while a friend took a picture from behind. The picture was made into a poster, and the caption of the poster reads:

Expose Yourself to Art

Now just image yourself wearing a trench coat, standing before a gnarly piece of code while a friend takes a picture. This poster could be titled:

Expose Yourself to New Ideas

You'll be a much better debugger for it.

The Best Bugs Are the Ones that Aren't There

Debugging starts sooner than most programmers think. The easiest debugging is the debugging you don't have to do. Recall what I said earlier about finding bugs: it takes much more effort

7

to find bugs than to fix them (but there will always be bugs that drive good programmers insane). Add both efforts together, and you will see that it is almost always worth the time to get it as good as possible in the first place.

Tip: A bug saved is a bug earned.

Efficient Debugging

One very efficient debugging method is to let the program itself tell you there's a bug. C compilers come with a great little macro—assert()—that you can use to tell you if something is wrong.

It's simple to use:

```
assert( <a condition that evaluates to true or false> );
```

For example, if you have a function that requires non-null values, a simple statement such as

```
assert( val !=NULL );
```

is just the ticket. If a null value crops up, you see the following:

```
Assertion failed: expression, file (filename),
    line (line number)
```

As you can see, you still have to debug to find the source of the problem. At the very least, you know there is a problem.

While good debugging tools go a long way toward making debugging an almost reasonable thing to do, *how* you think has even more to do with it. Of course, I'd rather have a nice symbolic, mixed-language debugger with multiple windows any time I can get one.

Tip: Follow the line of least resistance.

When you're debugging, it's easy to get lost in the details. If you try to track every possibility, you'll spend gobs of time and you won't get very far. If you are forced down to the assembly level, you can spend enormous amounts of time (especially if you aren't an expert). So, if you're writing down a list of addresses on a pad, and the list grows to more than ten addresses, you're probably not using the right approach to solve the problem. Try something else!

The principle problem in debugging is to observe the bug as it happens. It's a great feeling when you can step through and watch data being destroyed before your eyes. The way it usually works, however, is that you arrive somewhere in the code and the data have already been destroyed. Then you have to think back to where the destruction might have occurred. That's the tough part. Did it happen in your code? Did it happen in a tool you built? Did it happen in a tool someone else built for you? Did it happen in a commercial tool you use? Did it happen somewhere in the operating system? Or was this bad data the result of other bad data—is the code fine?

The list of questions is nearly endless. However, you can impose some structure on the process. Always (or almost always) assume that the bug is in the highest layer. Why?

Generalization: *The highest layer, being far removed from the guts of things, and understanding nothing of said guts, will sometimes try to do the impossible.*

These kinds of bugs are pesky but manageable. They do involve some redesign because they imply that the highest layer is misusing the lower layers, or that the lower layers are not providing a needed service to the highest layer. Those kinds of problems, however, are easier to find (there's less code at the highest layer; it sits on all the other layers) and often easier to solve (the higher-level code is not machine-specific).

Like all generalizations, this one has its weak spot. Certain kinds of bugs—freeing memory too soon, walking off the end of an array—are inherently low-level. The best place to catch these is in module testing, but you have to develop your own sense of the difference between the symptoms of high- and low-level bugs.

If the bug is not in the highest layer, go down one layer or so and see what's going on there. As you drop down layer by layer, you increase the complexity of the debugging effort. Examining lower layers adds more code, and the code tends to get more technical and less readable (by humans) at the lower levels. At some level you start hitting code written by others, either project tools or commercial products. The difficulty level takes a

7

quantum leap at that point. Not only do you have to debug, you have to figure out why things were done the way they were. All those nice, comfortable assumptions you can make about your own code aren't there.

What? You made assumptions about your own code? Egad! Oh no!

Rule: Don't make assumptions about your code.

Just because you *think* you've found the perfect way to handle something doesn't mean you *have* found it. Just because a section of code performs flawlessly for months doesn't mean it will continue to perform so admirably. How many times have you said to yourself as you were debugging, "I can skip over this part; it's fine," only to discover hours later, when you finally step through "that part" and find the bug, that you were dead wrong. Be honest, now. We've all done it.

Using the Right Tools

It's hard to give advice in this arena because we're talking about the entire world of ANSI C here. There are a number of compilers out there. Some come with a debugger, some don't. Various operating systems have debuggers—some are good and some are awful. Various vendors offer debuggers that work with a variety of compilers. Some debuggers tell you everything you ever wanted to know about the hardware you're running. Others are special-purpose debuggers designed to find particular kinds of problems.

Tip: Just because you've always used debugger A doesn't mean that debugger B might not be better, or faster, or have some useful features worth a closer look.

It's easy to get into a habit with debuggers. It can take a long time to learn all the nuances; debugging can easily get technical instead of friendly. Ultimately, there are always bugs that wedge themselves right down into the dirtiest parts of the code, right where code meets hardware. I can imagine them nesting in hardened little places right on the board.

7

The C language itself depends on the compilers that implement it. A bug on one platform might not be a bug on another. This kind of stubborn, low-level nastiness is one source of "unsolvable" bugs. Other sources include the complexity of certain operating environments (try debugging in Microsoft Windows on a PC if you want a fun time), unorganized code (perish the thought!), and poorly designed debuggers. It's hard to combat some of these, but if the tool you are using isn't getting the job done, expand your toolbox.

Documenting the Debugging Process: Is It Necessary?

I have a bone to pick. I have rarely seen a programming environment where there was communal debugging, and I think that's a shame. Debugging is often thought of as a lonely pursuit. One man, one machine, fighting against the demons of the code. Hogwash. There are two important ways to make everyone on a project a better debugger:

◆ Hold joint debugging sessions.

◆ Publish the results of debugging efforts.

There are several good ways to have joint debugging sessions:

◆ *Senior/Junior debugging.* This involves a joint effort between a more experienced team member and a less experienced team member. The junior party usually learns a lot about the code underlying the area under investigation, as well as a variety of useful debugging skills and strategies. The senior member gets to show off. If the junior member is good, he or she can use the distance from the specifics to make some nifty leaps of logic.

◆ *Team debugging.* This involves people with similar experience and related assignments working together on a piece of code. It uses the old "two heads are better than one" approach to solve a (usually) knotty problem. There is also bound to be some cross-fertilization of ideas.

♦ *Cross-team debugging.* This involves pulling together programmers from different parts of the project to debug. You can often solve the really thorny problems, the ones that involve vast sections of code, using this approach.

♦ *Test/programming debugging.* This approach is a favorite of mine: the tester who finds a bug works with a programmer to solve the problem. In this case, the tester learns more about what is inside the code, the tester and the programmer learn that the other one is human, and the tester gets a head start on his programming career. Some pooh-pooh this idea on the grounds that testing should be a black-box process, but there are so many testers who don't do this that the small number who do represent no threat to the black-box approach.

I'm not thoroughly convinced that a pure black-box approach to functional testing is that valuable anyway. Bugs do not play by any rules I've ever heard of—they do anything they have to do to get the software to break. My feeling is that if bugs can do anything they want, so can testers. If it finds bugs, it's a good approach to testing.

In situations where some form of joint debugging isn't practical, you can publish the results of individual debugging sessions (not each session, of course; no one wants to hear every detail of a six-hour effort with its 32 back-tracking runs and 63 false starts). The results of a debugging session are publishable if you learned something that is not generally known, but should be. It's a judgment call.

For example, if you are debugging a module that posts to a general ledger, you may discover that the process is sensitive to the length of one of the fields. If the field is longer than a certain value, it causes an overflow—either the incoming data has to be shortened, error checking has to added, or the field has to be lengthened. This is worth publishing for several reasons. Design issues

7

are involved—it's not immediately clear how to solve the problem. If there are other modules posting to the ledger, they will also encounter the bug. They may not hit the bug, however; that's important to know, too. Maybe you're not using the latest version of the tools. (Of course, if the last person who found this bug and fixed it had published, you would know that.)

How you publish is not a big issue—E-mail, fancy forms, whatever works in the local environment is fine.

8

Maintaining Code

8

The phrase "reusable code" has come into vogue recently. It is meant to be cutting-edge stuff, but we've had reusable code all along. The issues involved in reusable code—such as modularity, readability, and indifference to the caller—are exactly the issues involved in code maintenance. In fact, if all (or at least most) programmers paid more attention to code-maintenance issues, the whole field would be advancing more quickly.

Everything I've written up to this point has been focused right here, on this section of the book. The greatest waste of time and money in the computer industry occurs in the act of maintaining code (or in the act of throwing away unmaintainable code). Sloppy testing is a slow second.

Why is this true? There are a few reasons:

◆ *It's easier to code it to run than to code it for the ages.* Face it, getting code to run is a lot easier than making it readable and well organized—up to a point, that is. At some point, sloppy code starts to be difficult to write in "real time." The cure for this problem is to realize that code maintenance begins when the first bug occurs and you have to go back to your code to fix it.

◆ *Enforcing good coding practices is easier said than done.* It takes a volunteer bad guy to get out the whip and enforce good coding practices. It works best, of course, when each programmer sees to it that good practices are followed. There are two principles to follow to write good code: create libraries in layers, and write readable code.

◆ *The reward for maintainable code is far down the line.* The advantages of well-written, accessible code may not be realized until much later in the process—when it's time for a major upgrade or when a major flaw is discovered, or maybe it won't be long at all (perhaps you'll be too sick to work and someone else will have to handle your code while you're out).

The simple fact is that the rewards for good code far outweigh the costs. The problem is that human nature tends to be much more interested in now than later.

The User Is Just Half of Your Audience

8

I'll keep the propaganda for good coding practices flowing. When talking about the programmer over your shoulder, I considered the two audiences for your work: the user and the maintenance programmer. You need a mental image for the maintenance programmer that will inspire you to treat him or her with respect. One image that comes to my mind is that of the old Maytag repairman. He's got a kindly face, sort of like someone's uncle. It would be hard to be mean spirited toward such a kindly-looking old gentlemen. He's there to help you, right? In many ways, he is the audience you should be playing to when you write code.

In many cases, that maintenance man is you, the one who wrote the code in the first place. If you're running a one-person shop, the pressure to get it done—and now—can be enormous. There just aren't enough hours in the day, right? Wrong. There have got to be enough hours. Good, maintainable code is money in the bank!

How so? Look at it this way: the code you write represents an investment. You spend time to create it, and your time is your investment. What return are you getting on that investment? Thirty-five dollars an hour? Fifty? Twenty-five? Whatever it is, wouldn't you like to get more?

It's easy. Write code well the first time and use it again. The second time, your time investment is less, but to the customer the value of the code is the same, so you spend less to get the same income. This may seem obvious, but I have to point it out because so many programmers seem to not know how this works. Why else would they ignore such a gold mine? This way, your investment pays back not only in the short term, but in the long term as well.

There's another way your investment can pay you back: maintenance. If you are ever called in to make changes, you can quote an attractive figure that will discourage your customer from trying other sources. You'll actually see more business this way, not less.

8

All of this ignores what good code will do for your reputation, the greatest single investment every independent programmer has. Good coding practices will spread your name faster than any other mechanism, among both your fellow programmers (who know they can rely on you if they need help) and your customers (who will appreciate the reliability that seems to go naturally with well-commented, readable code). Funny how it works that way, but most successful programmers I have met work that way too.

Spaghetti Versus Lasagna

We've all heard of a bad piece of coding called "spaghetti." I maintain that there are two kinds of coding nightmares: spaghetti and lasagna.

The worst varieties of spaghetti code use lots of gotos and continues and wander all over the place. The code is neither well organized nor readable.

There is another flaw in programming that has nothing to do with organization or flow control. It is obfuscation, intentional or otherwise. I call this lasagna code. This code may be layered and organized, but it is as soft as ricotta, clear as tomato paste, and hard to digest. Such code consists of short or obscure variable and function names, tools that are undocumented, confusing internal and exported routines, and a general disregard for readability. Limit your lasagna to the restaurant, please. Otherwise, we'll all have to wear bibs while we program.

You Can't Maintain Bad Code, No Matter How Hard You Try

The section title says it all, doesn't it? *You can't maintain bad code, no matter how hard you try.* It's really that simple. I think of it as disposable code, the paper plate of programming (as long as we're

8

going with food metaphors). No shoes, no shirt, no service. No layers, no comments, no maintenance possible.

Being a Good Neighbor

Have we gone too far into the '90s to use a concept as simple as being a good neighbor? I hope not. No one codes in a vacuum. I have worked on projects that used abominable coding practices, and I have worked on projects with code that was elegant and supremely maintainable. Guess which was more fun?

No one, and no company, is immune to bad practices. Human natures tends to gravitate to the short term, remember? I know for a fact that several major software products—you've probably used some of the ones I'm thinking of—have source code that is impossible to maintain. The owners of that code are wondering how the heck to remain competitive. If they cared to ask, I'd have to say that the only viable route is to start over. I've yet to see a product stay competitive without a rewrite at some point.

The problem occurs at every level. There are small shops that have written code they can't maintain. There are software vendors who have shelved major custom applications that were dead before they were installed. There are PC applications that have no future—enhancements would snap the already-fragile code. There are UNIX-based commercial applications—accounting, order entry, you name it—with code so twisted that companies have to hire more and more programmers, who, out of frustration, quickly move on to other companies.

So be a good neighbor. Be considerate of the next programmer down the line. Expect others to be considerate too. Do your small part for better code.

All right, I'll get down off my soapbox and get back to "real" programming issues.

9

Be a Tool Builder

9

Primitive man succeeded by being a tool builder. He was slower than the other animals; he did not have strong, deadly jaws with sharp teeth; and he had to spend an inordinate amount of time protecting his young-uns. A keen mind replaced speed (an ambush is safer and easier); arrows, clubs, and axes replaced teeth; and stockades took care of the extended childhood.

Programmers face the same problems, and tools are still the answer.

Programming is slow if you don't use tools—you are constantly reinventing the wheel. How do you attack a problem? By gumming it to death? No—you use tools. As to the problem of extended childhood, computer games probably are a better solution for that.

I find a great deal of confusion on the subject of tools. The concept seems to float and waver from one programmer to the next. It means one thing here, another thing there.

What Is a Tool?

Definition: A tool is anything made of code that you can use with minimal or no modification to accomplish a task.

Simple enough. A little modification is allowed here and there. Anything more than that sounds more like development than tool using.

What is a good tool?

Definition: A good tool is one that saves time.

The time saved, of course, applies to coding, researching, debugging, testing, and maintenance. Unless a tool offers a net saving of time across at least several of these levels, the tool might not be worth the effort.

Oh. That's a lot harder.

Yup.

9

Clarence, the programmer over my shoulder, is smiling. It's those far-reaching kinds of considerations he likes to remind me of.

What Makes a Good Tool?

A good tool is a very valuable thing. I'll give you an example.

A friend of mine, whom I consider to be a very thoughtful, well-organized programmer, developed a tool a few years ago that serves as an excellent example. It has passed through several hands, and it has emerged as close to perfect as a tool can get.

The tool is a state-machine generator. A state machine itself is a programming device that switches from state to state based on a set of rules. It can be a very efficient method for handling some very complex situations.

The tool enables you to specify information about states and state transitions in a relatively simple text file, which you then feed to the tool. It outputs state tables (in standard header files) that can be combined with your code. It can perform many tasks.

The original task for which the state-machine tool was written involved user input on a PC. Using the tool, a programmer could specify the appropriate responses to various situations. Each state had an integer associated with it, and a switch statement was used to branch appropriately for each state.

One important thing to note about the tool is that it was a general-purpose tool, put to use in a specific situation. If it had not been for the immediate need, the tool would never have been developed.

The programmer had another choice at that point: he could have simply tried to solve the immediate problem without creating any kind of general-purpose tool. However, this programmer was the sort who looks to the long view, and he knew that a state-machine generator could come in handy in other situations down the road. He had no idea at the time what those might be. In effect,

9

he used the immediate need to justify the effort to build a general-purpose tool, even though it would have been faster to simply solve the immediate problem directly.

To be complete, this story must include a few tough facts. The first version of the tool was not documented at all, contained no comments in the source code, and had no bells and whistles whatsoever. Because the programmer took the time to create a general-purpose tool, he did not take enough time to make it pretty. But at least he now had the tool.

About a year later, while working on another product for the same company, my friend recalled the state-machine generator he had built. He had a similar input problem, this time on a UNIX platform (a Sun workstation). He ported the tool to UNIX, and it performed well. He took the opportunity to clean it up a little, but it still lacked full-dress regalia.

Another programmer was working on a project on the Mac platform, and the tool (as well as several others) was ported to that platform, although it saw very little use. It did receive a graphical front end, however.

The thing to note about this phase in the tool's life is that it was portable. Different programmers could use the tool on other platforms. Such easy portability is the ideal case; however, it is not always possible, or even necessary.

Several years went by without any use for the tool. Then along came a major project, much bigger than anything my friend's company had ever worked on before. It just so happened that this project was on the PC platform, the tool's original home. In fact, again there was a need to create state machines to handle user input processing. This time, however, the situation was more complex. The original tool would have to be beefed up if it was going to be useful.

One of the ways a state machine decides what state to move to is to use transition terms. A transition term usually is a logical entity; if it is true, the switch goes one way, and if it is false, the switch goes another way.

An example of a transition term for text input is READ_ONLY. For example, if the Delete key is pressed and the transition term READ_ONLY is true, the state machine might go to the state BEEP to sound an alarm. If the READ_ONLY term is false, the state machine goes to the DELETE_CHARACTER state.

The complexity of the new problem was such that a tremendous number of transition terms were required to control movement from state to state. If this had been the Interstate Commerce Commission, the size of the bureaucracy would have choked all attempts at transportation.

So the way that the state machine was built changed. Instead of assigning an integer to each state, a function could now be associated with each state. This function could do anything it wanted, but usually it was a handler for the state. State machines could share handlers this way. It was a much more efficient method of dealing with the problem.

Several other changes were made as well. Instead of being limited to discrete state machines, one could now layer state machines, and machines could share transition terms. Simple conventions were used to distinguish local and remote terms—uppercase for local, lowercase for remote.

Fact: Tools need to evolve as you gain experience in your field.

As an aside, the state machine was modified to allow input via an event handler. Any event could now be used to initiate a state change, not just keystrokes.

And, at long last, the state-machine generator got its documentation. It was now being used by more than one person, so it was essential.

It was at this point that I got involved with the state machine. I was a writer, so I got to write the documentation. I was so fascinated with the power of the tool that I decided I had to try using it before documenting it. Let the record show that it enabled me to create a dynamite Battleship-style game in record time. As I've said, a good tool should prove useful in new and unanticipated contexts.

9

The interface of the state machine is simple and effective. The states are defined in a text file. A state-machine generator reads the text file and outputs header files and source code to use in your program.

A state machine can be very handy in a surprising variety of situations. I used my friend's tool in several of those situations. One was a simple text editor. There was a waiting-for-keystroke state, as well as states such as copying, moving, inserting, and so on. Control passed from state to state, and functions were called at many of the states. It was an elegant, well-organized way to get a job done.

Toward the end, as the state-machine generator became fairly mature, stylistic rules of usage began to develop; it had grown in all the major ways it needed to, and changes were reduced to nitpicking details. The style rules included such things as removing `if` statements from the functions called by the state machine, and enforcing all decisions into the state machine.

Many advantages accrue from using the state-machine tool. The two most important are smaller code size and faster execution speed. A very big advantage of this tool is that it enforces logical thinking about problems. It is as close to ideal as any tool I've seen.

Propaganda: A good tool enforces clear, logical thinking about the problem it is used to solve.

This is important. A tool that doesn't do this certainly is useful, but not as useful as it could be. A problem that is well understood invariably gets a well-coded solution.

Rule: The better you understand the problem, the better the solution you can provide.

The state-machine tool illustrates this perfectly. If my friend had not insisted, right at the beginning, that a general-purpose tool be built to solve an immediate problem, the elegant, multi-use solution would never have been created.

There is one further chapter in the story of the state machine. My friend's company recently began another project. This time it was in C++, not plain C, but our friend the state machine proved useful once again. The project involved databases, and there was a need to construct complex views of tables. Even more complex than the views themselves were the rules for updating the involved files. Some files were read-only, some were required, some were optional, some could have records added, and some couldn't. The programmer assigned to the task was having a hard time tracking all the variables. His code had gotten quite fragile—that is, a change in one area led to bugs in another area.

The state machine was hauled out one more time. Within a day, the basic rules had been coded and the code converted to run as a state machine. The logical requirements of the state machine assisted the programmer in organizing the facts at hand. Because every state must lead to another state, he had no choice but to consider all aspects of the system; anything left unconnected would be immediately obvious.

To quote my friend about the state-machine tool: "If you look at the history, there are a number of problems it solved. All but the original problem were unanticipated. It enabled us to share code, to save code size, to control database updates, and it even proved to be a real memory saver in one critical memory environment. It was never envisioned as being able to do most of those things."

I'd say that's a good description of the value of a tool constructed rigorously, updated thoughtfully, and always envisioned within a larger context.

Building Good Tools

Where do you start? As Julie Andrews suggested in *The Sound of Music,* "Let's start at the very beginning...."

Good tools start with a problem that needs to be solved. You cannot possibly build a good, useful tool without a thorough understanding of the problem at hand.

The problem has two aspects: the immediate need and the global considerations. The state-machine tool, discussed earlier,

9

hints at these two sides of the problem. In every case, you need to balance the immediate need against the global requirements.

Analyzing the Immediate Need

This is the part you probably already know how to do, because it is what you have been doing since the first time you wrote a program.

What you might not have been doing is looking for a way to get from the immediate problem to the larger issues. The first step in doing so is probably obvious, but I'll state it just in case:

Rule: Look for patterns in the immediate situation.

For example, if you need to provide masks for input of sample dates, there is an obvious pattern depending on where in the world you live. One pattern looks like this:

MM/DD/YY

Or, in many European countries, it looks like this:

DD/MM/YY

Or perhaps it needs to look like this:

DD.MM.YY

There are patterns, and there are larger patterns. The basic date is a pattern of characters; the collection of date formats is a larger pattern. But there is a still larger pattern as well. What we are really talking about is the existence of literal constants in the midst of variable data.

Eureka! We have made the jump from the immediate need to the global issue. Doing that is the secret to writing the very best of tools.

Analyzing the Global Issues 9

As soon as you have identified the global aspects of the problem, it is time to reflect. Have you indeed identified the scope of things? Are there other global issues worth considering?

Look at the preceding example concerning dates. The global issue has been identified as follows:

Issue: The need to provide input with both literal constants and variable data.

Is anything else going on here? Maybe. What about validating those dates? Or validating zip codes and area codes and whatever else you might come up with?

You need to choose how to deal with data validation. You can incorporate it right into your tool, but that's too close to hardcoding. What if you add other data formats later?

You could leave a "hook" for the data validation routines. You could have your tool check to see whether you told it that a data validation routine exists, and your tool could see that it is called, and that the data is passed to it.

You might want to make some rules for the data validation routine to follow. You might want to specify how you intend to pass the data to it; you might make rules about how the data validation routine can tell you whether the data is valid. (Maybe true and false are good enough, and maybe you want to pass an error message or a help message back from the data validation routine.)

There are a lot of questions to answer. But they must be answered if you are going to write a tool that will be useful for general situations. Your tool might interface with a wide variety of data validation routines. Perhaps someone somewhere down the line will get the idea that, well, if I can call a data validation routine, why can't I call a data-altering routine as well? If I don't consider that—and it might be quite a valid thing to do, if the data is invalid—perhaps the data validation routine knows just how to fix it. Shouldn't it have a way to do that?

9

There will always be more questions to answer. Practicality requires that you stop, at some point, and create, test, and publish the tool. As you learn—and as your tool has more experiences out there in the world with other programmers—the tool will advance and grow and get better and better. Someday, it might even be the perfect tool. But don't count on it.

10

C

The Programmer's Checklist

10

There are many ways to make an error when you are programming. After all, only a perfect program has no errors, and human beings are just not designed for perfection.

I have found that keeping a checklist of the worst sorts of errors, at least the more common ones, helps to control the fallout from stupid errors. Therefore, I offer my list of things to watch out for. Following the discussion of each item is a ready-for-photocopying page with the checklist in brief form.

Compare Function Arguments with Function Declarations

The data types of the arguments you use in function calls must match the data types that were declared with the functions.

You call several kinds of functions:

◆ Functions in the standard libraries (`strstr()`, `printf()`, and so on)

◆ Functions in your library

◆ Functions in project libraries

◆ Functions in commercial libraries purchased by you or your company

It goes without saying that you include the header file with the function declarations. Ahem.

There are several issues here. On the one hand, every function has a return type—either a data type or void. Make darn sure that the container you put this return value into is identical (no variations, no "they're almost exactly the same" comments) in type. An `int` is an `int`, a `long` is a `long`, and a `LEDGER_TABLE` is not a `TABLE`. Fuzzy return types equal fuzzy thinking, and that leads inevitably to the nearest bug. On the other hand, you are passing arguments to the function. Data type correspondence is just as critical. Pull no tricks, and cast only if you must.

As an aside, make sure that you declare your functions in useful ways. Make each argument name meaningful so that the declaration actually documents the function. I call it capsule documentation, and it is convenient. You can keep the header file open in one buffer of your editor and the source code in another. If you need to know what the function does, or if you need to verify an argument data type, it's right there at hand. If you don't have an editor that handles multiple buffers, get one. There's no excuse!

As another aside, keep a clear head about the difference between a declaration and a definition. A declaration is just that: it declares to all the world what something looks like. A function declaration, for example, appears in a header file and is included in many, many files. It tells the compiler what your function looks like, and the compiler uses that information to tell you whether you are using the function correctly. (You do allow your compiler to tell you when you use the wrong data type in a function, don't you?)

A definition, on the other hand, does the deed. The compiler makes sure that memory is reserved for the thing defined—a variable, a function, and so on. Each thing can have only one definition. If you have two or more definitions, you had better hope your linker is smart enough to tell you about it.

Initialize Variables

This is easy. If you define a variable, make sure it gets initialized. This is critical for pointers, as discussed in the section titled "Watch Out for Null Pointers."

You don't ever want to be caught using random data. You should always know that there is a valid value in a variable when you use it.

Match Opens and Closes

Obvious, right? If you have a left parenthesis, match it with a right parenthesis. If you put a curly brace at the beginning of a for, put

10

one at the end too. You knew this, right? There's nothing more embarrassing than a compiler that knows you can't count to two.

If You Allocate, So Shall You Free

I have a theory. It says that at least half of all bugs in major software products occur because of memory that wasn't freed properly.

I worked at a major (and long-since sold to the highest bidder) software company some years ago. There was an ace programmer on the staff who could code anything. Some people working for him were way over my head. However, there were so many memory problems in the product from careless allocations schemes that he had to be reassigned to debugging them. It is not good when your best brain spends months pulling out memory errors that should never have occurred in the first place. I strongly recommend that you include a table or list of allocations (unless your design permits stack-like allocations). You are tempting fate if you try to keep track of allocations by hand—no matter how small your application is.

However you deal with memory, you must have an overall scheme for its allocation and deallocation. You must know, for a fact, that every byte allocated will be freed—no exceptions!

Don't Use an Array Index That Doesn't Exist

Another rich source of bugs are loops that iterate past the end of an array—especially strings. The moment you write to the past-the-end memory, you are igniting a time bomb. It might blow now or later, but it will blow.

10

Variable Definitions on Top

Put your variable definitions at the top of your function, and put some white space between them and the first line of runnable code. While you are at it, comment every one of those suckers for the next time you have to look at the code. They have to be at the top, anyway; that's how C works.

Verify Loop Control

Loops are good bug factories. Every loop has three things you can check quickly to verify proper operation:

◆ Look at how the variable that controls the loop is initialized. Is it initialized to the correct value? Is it initialized at all?

◆ Where in the loop do you test the variable? Is the test accurate? Does it allow one too few, one too many, or just the right number of iterations? Did you remember to test the variable?

◆ How do you modify the variable in the loop? Is the modification properly controlled? Is the variable incremented at the right point in the loop? Is it incremented by the right amount, and in the right direction?

Escape Characters

The `printf()` and `scanf()` functions, among others, are frequent users of escape characters—things such as \n and \\. Every time you use one, take a moment to reflect on whether you used it correctly. You will avoid a lot of unpleasant surprises later.

10

Spaces in Macro Definitions

When you define a macro that takes one or more arguments, you must not put a space between the macro name and the first parenthesis. If you do, everything to the right of the space becomes what the macro will substitute.

For example, if you are defining a macro that will give you the larger of two arguments, the correct way to define the macro is

```
#define MAX(a,b) ((a)>(b)?(a):(b))
```

The arguments are enclosed in parentheses because one never knows what is going to be passed as an argument, and anything enclosed in parentheses will be evaluated as a single entity by the compiler.

If you use the macro in code like

```
MyVal = tan(MAX(a_vect, b_vect))
```

it gets expanded to this:

```
MyVal = tan(a_vect>b_vect?a_vect:b_vext)
```

But if you define the macro with a space before the parenthesis, such as

```
#define MAX (a,b) a>b?a:b
```

it expands to

```
MyVal = tan((a,b) a>b?a:b)
```

which does no one any good.

Multi-Line Macros

Did you know that you could create multi-line macros? Neither did I—at least not until I had spent several years coding in C. I mention them here both as a caution and as a suggestion. Be very careful with multi-line macros, because it is easy to make a mistake that can be very difficult to track down later. The only way to find the error is to instruct your compiler to generate a list of expanded code for you to look at.

On the other hand, there are times when nothing but a multi-line macro will work. For example, if you find yourself defining certain sets of variables in functions over and over, you might want to use a multi-line macro to ensure that all such definitions are identical.

Case Sensitivity

C is a case-sensitive language. Don't ever forget that! Many, many missing variables have just one or more letters in the wrong case.

Use of *const*

If you go around defining constants, why not protect them? An overwritten constant is just as capable of destroying vital memory as any other overwritten piece of memory.

Instead of coding

```
int a = "Constant"
```

try

```
const int a = "Constant"
```

This tells the compiler to let you know if you misuse the constant.

This is also very handy in function declarations. Suppose you have a function that returns a constant (perhaps it's from a lookup table). Declare the return type of the function with const:

```
const int MyFunction(char *argument1, int argument2)
```

Again, your compiler will now warn you if you try to assign the const to something that isn't declared const. It's like working with a safety net.

10

Semicolons After *for* and *while*

When you are writing C code, you get into the habit of putting a semicolon at the end of every line. Every once in a while, you will construct the opening line of a for or a while loop and stick a semicolon after it. Because there are no statements to execute within the loop (your intended code is just a block of code that will be executed once), you get distinctly unexpected behavior. The for loop will at least exit after the correct number of iterations, but the while loop will go on until you pull the plug.

Null-Terminated Strings

This goes without saying, right? Put a null at the end of your strings. Granted, you sometimes work with non-null-terminated strings, but they are the exception.

"C" Versus 'C'

"C" is a string of length one, terminated with a null character. The total memory used is two bytes. 'C' is a character data type, exactly one byte long, and there is no null terminator. Is that clear?

Watch Out for Null Pointers

Null pointers are the bane of C programming. Consider the following definition:

```
int *ptr;
```

This allocates memory for a pointer to type int. If it is a global variable, the contents of this memory are null. That is, initially the pointer points to nothing. It waits for you to make it point to something. If it is a local variable, it contains whatever was there before—the memory location might not even exist.

The problem arises when you fail to point the pointer at anything, and then use it anyway. Your code doubtless assumes that its pointers are pointing at something.

Strictly speaking, a null pointer is pointing at something: whatever sits at memory location 00000000 (16-bit address). It can be all kinds of things, but it is not what you expected. And if you change it, well, who knows what might happen on all the different platforms out there?

The rule is simple:

> **Rule:** *Always point your pointers at some valid data; don't leave them hanging for even one line of code lest you forget.*

So, when you do something such as free(p), it is always safest to follow it with p=NULL so you don't accidentally use it. (If you do, you'll catch it with an asert(p), right?)

continue and *goto*: Danger!

There can never be enough warnings about the use of goto and continue in C code. I don't know why it was thought necessary to add them to the language; everything else is so elegant and simple and readable that they sort of stand out like ugly ducklings. Unfortunately, they are never going to grow into handsome swans.

For the unconverted, let me explain. The goto statement can turn even the best-organized, most well-written code into spaghetti or lasagna. Following code with gotos is like trying to navigate the streets of Mexico City without a map. (If you haven't been there, it's hard even with a map.)

Think about it for a moment: you are tracing through the code, trying to make sense out of what's in front of you. All of a sudden, you see the statement

```
goto label;
```

Now you are lost. Where is label? What does it do? The primary tenet of readable C code—confining the code to small, readable

10

modules—has been violated. Suddenly, you cannot follow the code easily. Suddenly, the rug has been pulled out from under you.

Rule: If there is any way to avoid a goto *in your code, do so.*

The continue statement is not as egregious a violation of readable code as the goto, but it has a similar problem: it interrupts the flow of code in a way that disrupts readability. It is a hassle to deal with at the maintenance stage, and it is well worth avoiding if you can do so.

Operator Precedence

The various C operators have different levels of precedence. Knowing which comes first is important when you are constructing complex statements. A list of operators, arranged in order of precedence, appears in Table 14.5 of Chapter 14, "Operators and Expressions."

For example, consider the statement

```
result = *ptr * 2 + PriorResult^2 ? i[x]++ : --j
```

Operator precedence means that the compiler will see his statement as

```
result = ((*ptr * 2) + (PriorResult^2)) ? (i[x]++) :
    (--j)
```

Note that the * used as an indirection operator has higher precedence than the * used to indicate multiplication.

Rule: When in doubt, use parentheses. (They're cheap.)

= Versus == in *if* Statements

This is a common error. If you use a single equals sign in an if statement, you make an assignment rather than a comparison. For example,

```
if (TestVariable = TestValue) ...
```

sets `TestVariable` equal to `TestValue`. Thus, the result is always true, and the statements in the `if` will always be executed.

On the other hand, to test correctly:

```
if (TestVariable == TestValue) ...
```

This compares the two variables, and the code will be executed only if they are identical. Nothing changes in value as a result of the test.

Give a *case* a *break*

Each `case` in a `switch` statement must encounter a break statement before it will exit the `switch`. Here is an example of a correct `switch` statement:

```
switch (var)
{
  case 'S':
   DisplayString(OutData);
   break;
  case 'D':
   DisplayDate(OutData);
   break;
  default:
   BadVar(var);
}
```

Note that a break statement occurs for each case.

Rule: In a `switch` *statement, execution continues until a* break *statement is encountered.*

At times, you might want to deliberately avoid using a break statement so that several cases will share the same code:

```
switch (var)
{
  case 'S':
  case 's':
   DisplayString(OutData);
   break;
  case 'D':
  /* Fall through... */
  case 'd':
```

10

```
  DisplayDate(OutData);
  break;
 default:
  BadVar(var);
}
```

Of course, if you forget to put a `break` statement where it belongs, you will get unexpected results from your `switch` block. Sometimes, however, the error can be quite subtle. It's good practice to confirm flow in `switches` by eye before you compile. Think of it as part of your standard (boring, but necessary) preflight check.

Tip: Check every `switch` code block to make sure you have all the `breaks` in the right places.

Control Your *extern*

You can declare variables and functions as often as you like, because declarations are nothing more than information to the compiler about the data types involved. But you can define things only once, because a definition causes memory to be reserved.

Thus, if you say

```
char *buffer;
```

outside of a function, you can never say it again. Naturally, within functions you can repeat variable names because they represent different entities.

Rule: For a specified scope you can have only one entity with a specified name.

All other declarations of the variable buffer must be of the form

```
extern char *buffer;
```

You can even use `extern` inside a function, but don't.

Complex Declarations

10

At some point in your programming career, you will encounter someone else's complex declaration or you will need to construct your own. A complex declaration is one that includes a mixture of two or more of the following items:

◆ Indirection operator

◆ Array index

◆ Function parentheses

The key to reading or constructing a complex declaration lies in understanding how to read pointers. Unlike the English language, pointers are read from right to left, not from left to right.

Rule: Read pointers from right to left.

For example, the most basic pointer declaration

```
int *data
```

is read as "A pointer to data of type int." If the declaration is complicated a little,

```
int *data[3];
```

is read as "An array of three pointers to data of type int."

If a function is involved, as in

```
char *GetResult()
```

then it reads "A function that returns a pointer to data of type char."

On the other hand,

```
char (*GetResult)()
```

is read as "A pointer to a function that returns data of type char."

Rule: Read inside parentheses from left to right.

Consider a more complex declaration:

```
char *(*(*GetInput[x])())();
```

10

I'll arrange it for visual inspection:

```
char * ( * (*GetInput[x])() )();
```

This gives "an array of *x* pointers to functions that return pointers to functions that return pointers to values of type char."

A word of caution about complex declarations:

Tip: Don't use a complex declaration unless you have absolutely no choice.

Frequently, you can use typedefs to clarify such expressions; doing so also enforces consistency. The next programmer down the line would much rather see a clearly constructed typedef than a monster such as that last example.

The C Programmer's Checklist

10

❏ Compare arguments with function declarations.

❏ Initialize all variables.

❏ Match opens and closes.

❏ If you allocate, so shall you free.

❏ Don't use an array index that doesn't exist.

❏ Put variable definitions at the top of the function and separate them with white space.

❏ Verify loop control: initialization, testing, and modification of the variable.

❏ Check to see whether escape characters are correct.

❏ Don't put spaces in macro definitions.

❏ Double-check multi-line macros.

❏ Beware of case-sensitivity pitfalls.

❏ Use const to control data changes.

❏ Check for extraneous semicolons after for and while.

❏ Null-terminate strings.

❏ Check for "C" versus 'C' (string vs. character constant).

❏ Watch out for null pointers.

❏ Be aware of the dangers of using continue and goto.

❏ Verify operator precedence.

❏ Check for = versus == in if statements.

❏ Give every case a break statement.

❏ Control your extern.

❏ Double-check complex declarations.

11

C Some Practical Advice

11

There are certain constructs and operations in C that are worth spending some time discussing in greater detail. Face it—as elegant as C is as a language, there are some concepts that require more subtle attention than others.

The good news is that these sections are the ones that give C its great power as a language. Like anything powerful, you must pay attention to the details to get the degree of control you need to utilize the power.

Macros Are Really a Form of Documentation

Macros are an overlooked art in C programming. Most beginner programmers take macros for granted and never look very far beyond the ability to #define simple substitution macros. You can go a lot further with macros than you think, but the further you go, the murkier the waters get, and the greater attention you must pay to the rules.

The simplest macros are #define statements like these:

```
#define DEFAULT_HANDLE      0
#define INV_FILE            "inventry"
#define DEFAULT_EXTENSION   "txt"
#define INV_HANDLE          DEFAULT_HANDLE + 1
#define READ_ONLY           0x0001
```

Notice that the fourth #define statement in this list is a macro that uses another macro.

When the macro text is encountered in your program, the text you defined will be substituted. In other words, a statement such as

```
Handle = fileopen(INV_FILE, READ_ONLY);
```

is converted by the compiler to look this way

```
handle = fileopen("inventry", 0x0001);
```

before actually generating the code.

The primary advantage of such macros is that they enable you to define things in one place, and then use them as needed throughout your code. If you need to change it, you only have to change it in one place.

Macros can also take arguments. Many of the "functions" in the standard C library are actually macros. For example, putc() is actually a macro. Here is a typical definition for putc():

```
#define putc(c,file) \
(--(file)->_cnt>=0?(*(file)>_ptr++=(c)):_flsbuf(c,file))
```

The first argument to putc() is a character to be written to a file; the second argument is a pointer to an internal structure that contains the file information.

Note the use of the line continuation character (\) in this example. This enables you to continue a macro definition to another line. A macro can actually contain many statements.

Another example of a standard library "function" that is really a macro is toupper. You might think it could be defined this way:

```
#define toupper(c) \
    ((c)>='a' && (c)<='z'? (c)+('A'-'a'):(c))
```

This would be a dangerous macro. Why? Consider how the statement

```
ch = toupper(ch++);
```

evaluates:

```
ch = toupper(((ch++)>='a' && (ch++)<='z'? (ch++)+('A'-
    'a'):(ch++)));
```

Do you see the danger? The expression ch++ is evaluated at least three times when the macro expands. This is not a desired behavior. That's why, in most implementations, toupper is defined this way:

```
#define toupper(c) ((c)+'A'-'a')
```

The expression is only evaluated once. However, the macro does not check to make sure you sent it a lowercase character for

11

conversion. If you want to avoid nonsense results, it is up to you to verify the data before calling the macro:

```
newc = islower(c) ? toupper(c) : c
```

A well-behaved macro only evaluates each argument once. A poorly-behaved macro should only be used with variables, not expressions. It is probably a better idea to stay away from poorly-behaved macros, period.

Putting a macro in a macro can create unwieldy expressions. Many macros expand to quite a large number of characters. Using a macro as the argument to another macro can result in huge expressions. That's not so bad when you are writing the code, but it can make for complex debugging and maintenance.

It can be tempting to use macros instead of type definitions. When it comes to pointers, you will quickly see that this is not a good idea.

Consider the following definition:

```
#define LEDGER_TABLE struct table *
```

When you try to use it to declare several variables, you run into a problem:

```
LEDGER_TABLE receivables, payables;
```

expands to

```
struct table * receivables, payables;
```

The first variable, `receivables`, is (correctly) a pointer to a structure of type `table`, whereas the second variable, `payables`, is a structure instance, not a pointer. This situation is better handled by creating `LEDGER_TABLE` with a type definition:

```
typedef struct table LEDGER_TABLE;
```

In this case, it becomes legal to say

```
LEDGER_TABLE receivables, payables;
```

and both variables will be pointers to structures of type `table`.

Arrays, Structures, and Pointers

11

These three items can be said to represent the heart of the C language. Mastery of these three topics will give you the tools you need to become an advanced programmer.

Arrays

In many ways, arrays and pointers are the same thing in C. This may not be obvious, however, unless you look at the physical representations in memory. Nonetheless, as you will see, arrays are accessed and manipulated using either array subscripts or pointers.

The syntax for declaring an array is simple:

```
int array[10];
```

defines an array of ten integers.

To access each element of this array, you could write the following:

```
for(i=0; i<10; i++)
   a = array[i];
```

This sets the variable a to each integer value in the array, one for each iterations through the for loop.

Note that the first element of the array has a subscript of *0* (zero), and the last element has a subscript of *9*. Using your fingers, you can quickly determine that this represents ten elements in the array.

Rule: Array subscripts start with 0 (zero).

Keep this in mind if you want to avoid embarrassing bugs.

There is another way to access the elements of an array, using pointers:

11

```
int *i;
for(i=array; i<array+10; i++)
   a = *i;
```

Since the variable array, used without a subscript, gives us the address of the beginning of the array (that is, the address of element 0), we can set i equal to that address in the for loop (i is also a pointer to type int, and we have an array of int's). We test i by making sure it is never any larger than "array + 10".

But what is the meaning of "array + 10"?

If you add a number n to a pointer to an array, the result is not the address of the array plus the number. The result is the address of the nth element of the array. It's a nifty trick, and it has a name: pointer arithmetic.

The same thing happens when we increment i: each time, i is incremented to point to the next element in the array.

An array is finite in length—it ends somewhere in memory. Whether you are incrementing an array subscript or a pointer, you must guard against incrementing too far. If you reference an element that does not, in fact, exist, you get exactly what you should expect: garbage. Incrementing past the end of an array is a common source of bugs, and one worth guarding against.

Structures

Structures exist to allow you, the programmer, to package dissimilar data types into one entity.

Tip: Think of a structure as a one-record database.

For example, if we were to create a structure for an order entry application, we would need to include the following information about the order itself:

◆ The order number

◆ The date of the order

◆ The customer number

◆ The salesperson ID

◆ The total of all items

◆ The freight charges

◆ Tax

◆ The total order, including goods, taxes, and freight

◆ A linkage to the detail items on the order

Each kind of information is stored as a different kind of data. For example, the order number could be an integer or a string; the total of all items would be a float, and so on. You obviously can't stick the information into an array, because an array must contain data of one specific type.

To declare a type definition for your structure, you might have something like the following:

```
struct ORDER_ENTRY
{
    int order_number;
    long order_date;
    char cust_number[11];
    char sales_ID[4];
    char ship_method[4];
    char packed;
    char back_ordered;
    char shipped;
    char returned;
    float item_total;
    float order_freight;
    float order_tax;
    float order_total;
    /* what about the detail linkage ?*/
}
```

You were doing fine until you came to the linkage to the order details. There are several ways that you can include the order details.

The most efficient way involves linked lists. Linked lists are always constructed using structures. To use a linked list, begin by putting a pointer into the structure. It points to a structure containing information about the first item on the order. The revised structure looks like this:

```
struct ORDER_ENTRY
{
    int order_number;
    long order_date;
    char cust_number[11];
    char sales_ID[4];
    char ship_method[4];
    char packed;
    char back_ordered;
    char shipped;
    char returned;
    float item_total;
    float order_freight;
    float order_tax;
    float order_total;
    struct ORDER_ITEM *item;
}
```

Naturally, you must define a structure of type ORDER_ITEM:

```
struct ORDER_ITEM
{
    int item_number;
    int quantity;
    float price;
    ORDER_ITEM *next_item;
}
```

Note that the structure for an item contains a place to put a pointer to the next item. If there is no next item, the value is null.

Thus, you put a pointer to the first item in the order structure, and you put a pointer to the next item in each item. As long as you know where to start, you can easily navigate the list. Of course, you have to take care of allocating memory for each structure, and some other nice details, but consider that your homework.

Pointers

Ah, pointers. I love pointers. I love them for two reasons:

◆ I felt an enormous amount of satisfaction when I finally achieved a gut-level understanding of pointers;

11

◆ They are incredibly useful.

It took me about a year to get pointers into my bloodstream. I think it took me so long because I was too proud to ask someone to sit down with me and explain them. Don't repeat my mistake. It is not possible to write first-class C code without mastering pointers, and you don't want to have to wait a whole year for that, do you?

The concept of pointers is easier to work with than the notation used to represent pointers, so I'll start with concepts and move to notation in a moment. A pointer is simply a variable that points to something else. It is the nature of computers that "something else" resides in memory, and the way to point to it is to use its address. Thus, pointers are inextricably entwined with addresses. This enables us to state an obvious, but important, truth:

Rule: A pointer always contains an address.

Abandon that rule at your peril! If you set one pointer equal to another pointer, you are merely copying the contents of the pointer. Thus, you are simply copying an address from one container to another container. You now have two copies of an address. This means that the two pointers now point to the same thing. There are not two copies of data; there are two copies of an address.

Rule: Copying a pointer copies an address, not the thing addressed.

Now consider pointer notation is some detail. The asterisk is used with a pointer variable name like *p to indicate the thing pointed at. In other words, if you say p, you mean "the address contained in the variable p." If you say *p, you mean "the contents of the address contained in the variable p." It is very important that the type of the pointer p be the same as the type of the contents.

Rule: Don't mix types between pointer and data.

This notation, although a bit obscure and certainly not intuitive, is nonetheless quite handy in terms of the power it gives you. Consider a pointer to a function. Because a function resides

11

at an address in memory, you can point to that address and, in effect, pass a function around in arguments just like data. That is powerful stuff!

Pointers are also useful when working with large data structures. Structures can be quite large, and it would be very time consuming to try to pass a complete copy of a structure between functions. It is much faster to pass around a pointer to the structure instead.

While I was writing this book, I received mail via CompuServe, asking me if I would clarify the exact means used to pass pointers to functions:

I have yet to find a good reference on pointers and function calls. One of the problems I had trouble with as a beginner was passing a FILE pointer to a function. I wanted to pass the pointer to a function and have the function open the file and update the file pointer so that the calling function could use it.

Eugene H. Wheeler Jr.

Well, Eugene, I would hate to think that there are no good references on this question, but just in case that is true I want to include it here.

You could, of course, use open() to open the file; it returns an int, so no pointers to structures are involved. But take the bull by the horns here and use fopen(), which returns a pointer to a FILE structure. Here is the function that does the opening of the file:

```
FILE *MyOpen(char * filename)
{
    return fopen(filename,DEFAULT_MODE);
}
```

Hey, it doesn't take a FILE pointer as an argument. Well, this is one way to deal with the problem, you see. Instead of passing the FILE pointer as an argument, just call the function in your code like this:

```
FILE *my_file;
/* ... */
my_file = MyOpen("filename.ext");
```

11

Of course, that's a lot like using fopen yourself, except that you provide a default file mode. The idea is that you save the step of passing the extra argument. If you do want to pass the pointer to the function, then you must redefine the function like this:

```
void MyOpen(char * filename, FILE *f)
{
    f = fopen(filename,DEFAULT_MODE);
}
```

Note that there is no return value. You can call the revised function like this:

```
FILE *my_file;
/* ... */
MyOpen("filename.ext", my_file);
```

Pointers on Pointers to Pointers: Indirection Mastered

The real fun with pointers begins when you consider a pointer to a pointer. In other words, start with a container. This container holds an address. The address it holds points to another container. This other container also holds an address, and the address it holds points to some actual data.

Why would anyone want to do such a thing? I'm glad you asked; it gives me a chance to tell my favorite pointer war story. In the days when I was just beginning to learn to work with C, I encountered a problem that was very difficult for me to solve. I was pretty much on my own with it, because the other programmers on the team were all working on a tight deadline. At that point, I wasn't even an official C programmer, so asking for help was out of the question.

I labored mightily, and came up with a piece of code perhaps a hundred lines long. I won't repeat the code here; it would be too embarrassing as well as a waste of space. The code was slow, ungainly, and I had a feeling there was a better way to solve the problem.

11

The problem was that, given a list of strings in memory, I wanted to look at each string in turn. The strings were null terminated and arranged at various places in memory. There was an array of pointers to the strings. I asked a friend who, like me, was an aspiring C programmer. He wasn't much help, but he had a friend in a different department who was willing to help novice programmers learn the ropes. (If you are a novice, find such a person and stick to him or her like glue. If you are an experienced programmer, find a novice and hand him or her a glue pot.)

Tip: Other programmers are your best source of information.

This friend of a friend laughed (kindly, I think) when I told him about my problem. He wrote just two lines of code on a white board for me, and it changed my life.

Let me set the scene. The array of pointers to the strings was called strings. The last element of this array was, conveniently, a null pointer, giving me a convenient way to know when I had found the last string. Here's what he wrote on the board:

```
for(ptr = strings; *ptr!=0x0000; *ptr ++)
    MyStringFunction(*ptr);
```

This simple loop walks through each pointer in the array of pointers to strings, and passes it to my function, which can do anything it wants with the string it gets. It replaced nearly a hundred lines of struggling code that I had written. I was so happy to see such an elegant solution that I never had the time to be embarrassed about my own poorly conceived code.

Here is a small program that illustrates the complete "pointer to a pointer" concept:

```
#include <stdio.h>

void MyStringFunction(char *string);

main()
{
    /* Define an array of pointers to strings. */
    char *strings[4];

    /* Define three strings. */
```

```
char *string1="This is string1.";
char *string2="This is string2.";
char *string3="This is string3.";

/* Define our pointer to a pointer to type char. */
char **ptr;

/* Put pointers to the three strings into our
   array. */
strings[0] = string1;
strings[1] = string2;
strings[2] = string3;
strings[3] = 0x0000;      /* Null pointer signifies no
                             more strings in array. */
```

```
/* Initialize ptr to the address of the array of
   string pointers. Stop when *ptr points to a null
   string. Increment by the length of one address in
   the array of pointers. */

for(ptr = strings; *ptr!=0x0000; *ptr ++)

   /* Perform an operation on the string
      pointed to. */
   MyStringFunction(*ptr);

   return(0);  /* Exit the program. */
}
```

```
void MyStringFunction(char *string)
{
   /* Display the passed string. */
   printf("The current string is: %s\n", string);
}
```

Take a closer look at what is happening in the for loop. When the for loop is first entered, three things happen.

```
ptr = strings;
```

First, you put the address of the array of pointers to strings into the variable ptr. This means that the variable ptr contains an address of (points to) a variable that is an array of pointers. It is thus a pointer to a pointer. At this point, it points to the address of the first string array (string1). Because ptr is not an array, it can only point to one element at a time.

11

```
*ptr!=0x0000;
```

This is the exit condition of the for loop. Note that here, the variable ptr is preceded by an asterisk (the indirection operator). You are saying that if the value at the address contained in ptr is zero, exit the for loop. Because you conveniently set the last element of the string array to zero, this works just fine.

```
*ptr ++
```

What are you incrementing here? Because ptr points to an array of pointers, you are telling the compiler you want to point to the next pointer in the array. This is the advantage of using a pointer to a pointer in this situation. By simply incrementing, you can walk through an array of pointers.

Inside the for loop, you pass a string to the function with the following line:

```
MyStringFunction(*ptr);
```

Because a string is passed to a function by passing a variable containing the address of the first character in the string, and because *ptr gives us the address contained in the current element of the array of pointers, you are, in fact, passing the string just the way you should. This concept, of course, works just as well with an array of pointers to any data type, even structures. In fact, such usage is probably more common, but I thought that using strings might make the concepts a little easier to approach.

Bitwise Operations: Practical Uses

First, let's review the bitwise operators.

>>	right shift
<<	left shift
~	ones complement
^	bitwise exclusive OR
&	bitwise AND
¦	bitwise OR

The right shift operator shifts the bits in a value to the right. Bit positions left vacant on the left side are assigned a zero value if the variable is unsigned (which is what you normally work with; shifting unsigned variables adds complications). For example:

```
value = 0x75;   /* 0000 0000 0111 0101 */
value >> 3;     /* 0000 0000 0000 1110 */
```

In some implementations, shifting right with a signed value shifts in a one; in others, it shifts in a zero. Where portability is an issue, stick to unsigned variables.

The left shift operator is simply the reverse of the right shift operator; it shifts the bits to the left. Bit positions left vacant on the right are assigned a zero value.

```
value = 0x75;   /* 0000 0000 0111 0101 */
value << 3;     /* 0000 0011 1010 1000 */
```

The ones complement operator switches the value of all bits: a one becomes a zero, and a zero becomes a one.

```
value = 0x75;   /* 0000 0000 0111 0101 */
~value;         /* 1111 1111 1000 1010 */
```

The exclusive OR operator is a comparison operator. It compares the bit values in two numbers. If a given bit position has different values in each number, it returns a one in that position. If a given bit position has the same value in each number, it returns a zero in that position.

```
value1 = 0x75;            /* 0000 0000 0111 0101 */
value2 = 0x175;           /* 0000 0001 0111 0101 */
value3 = value1 ^ value2; /* 0000 0001 0000 0000 */
```

The AND operator is also a comparison operator. It compares the bit values in two numbers. If a given bit position in both numbers contains a one, it returns a one for that position. All other positions will be zero.

```
value1 = 0x75;            /* 0000 0000 0111 0101 */
value2 = 0x175;           /* 0000 0001 0111 0101 */
value3 = value1 & value2; /* 0000 0000 0111 0101 */
```

The OR operator is also a comparison operator. It compares the bit values in two numbers. If there is a one in a given bit position

11

in either of the two numbers, it returns a one in that position. If there are zeroes in both numbers at a given position, it returns zero.

```
value1 = 0x75;              /* 0000 0000 0111 0101 */
value2 = 0x175;             /* 0000 0001 0111 0101 */
value3 = value1 | value2;   /* 0000 0001 0111 0101 */
```

The mechanics of the bitwise operators, as you can see, are pretty straightforward. What was always confusing to me, and what I will try to explain here, is why you would ever want to use something so arcane.

But before we go on to that, it's worth a moment of your time to consider one other important use of bits in the C language: bit fields in a structure.

There are times when you need to store information that really does not require a full byte. For example, if you are storing a simple yes or no, you really only need one bit. That bit can be set to *1* or *0*, respectively. But how do you set just one bit? If you could do that, you could cut your storage requirements from one byte per item to one bit per item—an eight-fold decrease. Bit fields provide us with this ability. There are other ways (which I will discuss in a moment), but bit fields provide the clearest source code, if not the fastest execution times.

Consider the structure example you used earlier:

```
struct ORDER_ENTRY
{
    int order_number;
    long order_date;
    char cust_number[11];
    char sales_ID[4];
    char ship_method[4];
    char packed;
    char back_ordered;
    char shipped;
    char returned;
    float item_total;
    float order_freight;
    float order_tax;
    float order_total;
    struct ORDER_ITEM *item;
}
```

You could use bit fields for the items in bold to compress the storage requirements:

```
struct ORDER_ENTRY
{
   int order_number;
   long order_date;
   char cust_number[11];
   char sales_ID[4];
   unsigned int ship_method:5;
   unsigned int packed:1;
   unsigned int back_ordered:1;
   unsigned int shipped:1;
   unsigned int returned:1;
   float item_total;
   float order_freight;
   float order_tax;
   float order_total;
   struct ORDER_ITEM *item;
}
```

The first five bits are used to store the shipping method; five bits gives us 25 possibilities, or 32 possible shipping methods (0 through 31). One bit each is used to indicate true or false for the concepts of packed, backordered, shipped, and returned. This is a total of nine bits, so it will take at least two bytes to store the information; the extra bits are ignored. Structures must break on byte boundaries. The actual data type used to store the bits is determined by the compiler; it varies from implementation to implementation. The exact amount of memory saved by using may vary from compile to compiler, because different compilers can use different sizes of variables.

What took eight bytes in the original now takes two bytes. If this is a commonly used structure, that could be a substantial memory savings.

Note that I used unsigned ints; it is always safe to use unsigned variables when working with bits, whether in bit fields or otherwise. It doesn't make sense to use a float because the meaning of bits in a float is different than in an int, long or char.

We could, of course, simply define a variable and use its bits ourselves. This is, in fact, a more efficient process at run time. You

11

have to make a choice between speed and readability. In the next section, I show you how to get at individual bits without using bit fields.

Practical Bits

One of the most common uses for the bitwise operators is to set, clear, and test individual bits.

A number of the standard C library functions use bits to determine what to do. For example, bits are used to determine the mode in which a file is opened—will it be read only, should it be created if it does not exist, and so on.

One of the problems with using bits is that the code can be a little dense to read. That irritates the programmer over my shoulder; Clarence is making faces at the thought of a chunk of code riddled with bitwise operators.

You can develop a simple bit-operation library to illustrate how you can make bit operations more pleasant. For example, assume that you have the task of setting, reading, and clearing the status byte from a hardware port. Assume that you are doing serial communication, and that the following information is put into a status byte:

bit 0	change in CTS (clear to send)
bit 1	change in DSR (data set ready)
bit 2	trailing edge detect
bit 3	change in receive line
bit 4	CTS (clear to send)
bit 5	DSR (data set ready)
bit 6	ring indicator
bit 7	received signal

You could, of course, use bit fields:

```
struct StatusByte
{
    unsigned int CTS_change:1;
    unsigned int DSR_change:1;
    unsigned int TrailingEdge:1;
    unsigned int REC_change:1;
```

```
    unsigned int CTS:1
    unsigned int DSR:1
    unsigned int ring:1
    unsigned int signal:1
}
```

Using bit fields, you can access the bit indicating that it is clear to send:

```
if (StatusByte.CTS)
{
    /* It is clear to send. */
}
```

This is clear, concise, and elegant.

Nonetheless, you may find that you require better performance, and so may go to reading the bits directly. To do so, you need a set of constants to use:

```
#define STAT_CTS_change     0x01
#define STAT_DSR_change     0x02
#define STAT_TrailingEdge   0x04
#define STAT_REC_change     0x08
#define STAT_CTS            0x10
#define STAT_DSR            0x20
#define STAT_ring           0x40
#define STAT_sginal         0x80
```

This gives you a convenient, readable way to refer to each bit position.

A byte that is used to contain the switchable bits is often referred to as a *flag byte*, and the bits as *flag bits*. You need a way to set the flag bits. The following macro does it for you (note the use of a bitwise operator):

```
#define SetBit(b,c)    ((c) ¦ (b))
```

The macro SetBit performs a bitwise OR operation with a char and one of our bit-position macros. For example, to set bit position six write the following:

```
result = SetBit(STAT_CTS, result);
```

This is not quite as simple and clear as using bit fields, but it is understandable. Macro substitution turns this statement into:

```
c = SetBit(((c) ¦ (0x10)));
```

11

Because the only bit equal to one in STAT_CTS is the sixth bit, OR is guaranteed to set this bit in the final result. The OR leaves all other bit positions as they were. If you had already set other bit positions to *1*, they remain set.

You can add two more macros—one to clear a bit and one to test the bit—as follows:

```
#define ClearBit(b,c)    ((c) ^ (b))
#define TestBit(b,c)     (((c) & (b) == 0))
```

You can use the TestBit macro in an if statement to test whether a certain bit is set:

```
result = GetStatusByte(input_port);
if (TestBit(STAT_CTS_changed, result)
{
    /* It's clear to send, so let's send! */
}
```

This if statement is less clear than the one with bit fields, but it is not unduly obtuse.

The left and right shift operators are really multiplication and division operators, respectively, when used with unsigned values (and you most commonly use them with unsigned values). If you shift to the left, you are really multiplying by powers of two. If you shift to the right, you are actually dividing by powers of two.

For example, consider the following:

```
value1 = 0x10 >> 2
```

Hex 10 (0x10) is actually 16 decimal, and 0001 0000 binary. If you shift two places to the right, you get 0000 0100, which is 4 (decimal or hex). You divided by 4, which is 2 squared (2^2).

Think Globally, Act Locally

It never hurts to be aware of the larger issues. The amount of time involved in sticking your nose into the rest of the project isn't an excuse to meddle in the affairs of other programmers, but it is the only way to make sure that you are not developing a Robinson Crusoe style of programming.

Rule: *No programmer is an island.*

The code that you write must always fit into a larger picture. That's true in many ways. Even if you are a one-person shop, writing code for your own customers, you still have to make sure that the program you write fits into the customer's world and the customer's needs.

Consider all the ways that your code fits into the larger picture:

◆ Your code must interface with other code.

◆ Your code must mesh with the overall design.

◆ Others will test your code (black-box testing).

◆ You will have to debug your code at some later point in time.

◆ You or someone else will have to maintain your code.

◆ Someone will use your code to do a job.

All of these connections to the larger world have an impact on how you code. From the immediate mechanics of meshing with other code, to the abstract and arbitrary considerations of the end user's needs, your code is being pushed and pulled in a variety of directions. There are no absolute answers; there is no perfect path of least resistance. The best you can do is be aware of the many ways that you and your code need to interact, and to do so responsibly.

Tip: *Think globally, and act locally.*

Rules to Code By

11

I spoke with a programmer friend who is one of the best C coders I know, and I asked him to summarize the basic rule for writing good code and to provide a few examples of code that solves some of the classic programming problems. This friend's name is Gary Wisniewski, and he is the president of Apex Software. The rules belong to Gary; the comments are mine.

Rule 1: Get something working.

For some of us, it's easy to get caught up in a designing frenzy and to forget that we've got to get some code written. In all art forms (and programming is certainly an art, Clarence says), an artist learns from practice. In this respect, programming is no different—after you get some code working, you will see things that were simply not visible in design mode. Physically (or, in the case of programming, electronically) putting things together creates new information and stimulates new ideas.

There's nothing wrong with taking the time to design, but if a proper dose of actual coding isn't put into the mix, an impractical design and an impractical piece of software could be the result.

Rule 2: Don't take the easy way out when a redesign issue arises.

After you get something working, you will undoubtedly discover that something in the design isn't working right. There will always be a temptation to find an easy way to solve the problem. Don't do it! You will save more time in the long run if you redesign the software. It may cost you some extra time right now, but down the road you will save a lot more time. For example, each time someone uses a library function that has been done right, time will be saved. When maintenance and debugging come up, time will be saved.

Rule 3: Never write the same routine twice.

Yes, *never.* That doesn't mean you shouldn't improve it. It means that if you're going to use a routine in two places, write it once for both places.

Rule 4: *When writing function prototypes, use argument names that fully describe the purpose of the arguments.*

This rule appears elsewhere in this book. If you create carefully thought-out arguments for your function prototypes, they become little self-contained documentors of the functions.

Rule 5: *Use* const.

If something is a constant, tell the compiler. Use const in your variable and function definitions to tell the compiler to warn you if you try to do too much with something that is not supposed to be "muckable."

Rule 6: *Don't sacrifice program functionality because something is hard to code.*

There will be times when you are challenged by a problem. Don't be tempted to simplify functionality just because it's hard to write. Take the time to learn what you need to know to do the job right.

Rule 7: *When you design a function, think about how you will use it, not how you will write it.*

It's very easy to start thinking about a function in terms of its implementation. The code does not define the function, but it can limit it. Code to the design; don't design to the code.

Rule 8: *Avoid predefined limits.*

Arbitrary limits are the bane of programming. Don't imagine that you can predict the future, and don't hem yourself in with limits you may someday regret. Simple examples of this abound in the programming world. One that comes to my mind involves dates. A compiler project assumed that dates could be implemented as long ints. It turned out that the design specification should have mentioned the need to do "date arithmetic" with fractional dates. By the time the flaw was discovered, all the code

11

already relied on the fact that dates were integers. Unfortunately, because of an assumption, a massive effort was required to make the change.

Rule 9: Learn algorithms and practice implementing them.

Good code must be readable, but it also has to run efficiently.

Rule 10: Don't fall prey to trial-and-error methods. Understand what is happening, even if it takes time to do so.

Although you can discover things by trial and error that you will discover no other way, if all you get is some code that runs, you haven't gone far enough. You need to stop and ask yourself, Why does this work the way it does? The answer may take time, but this the only way to grow as a programmer.

Rule 11: Mutual dependencies between libraries are to be avoided (entirely).

Although this subject was covered in an earlier section, it is important enough to repeat. By making sure that libraries communicate in only one direction, you can ensure that the entire code base has a well-defined structure and thus automatically avoid spaghetti by eschewing mutual dependencies. Remember: if anything in library A calls anything in library B, then nothing in B can call anything in A.

12

Closing Thoughts:
The Zen of Coding

12

This book has covered a lot of territory. Some of it has been technical, practical how-to-do-it information. Some of it has, I hope, inspired you to look differently not just at your code, but at how you code and how you fit into the larger picture.

Although I am not a practitioner of Zen, it has become fashionable to look at the Zen-like aspects of everything from motorcycle maintenance to tennis. The practice of Zen involves a reliance on intuition rather than rote memorization. In that sense, yes, there is a Zen of coding.

Coding exists in that large, interior world of the mind. I suspect that I am not the only programmer who has discovered that there is a certain discipline to writing good code. It is as though the pleasures of writing code are richest only on the other side of a line defined by careful reasoning, consideration for the interfaces (human and machine), and a willingness to organize thoughts until the entire structure crystallizes in the mind. These are the considerations that define the Zen of coding. You can find them only by making the day-to-day considerations so routine that you have the room to code a little higher, a little better, a little more completely than the last time.

The common image of a programmer is that of a nerd who ought to get a life. That notion is silly because it implies that programming has no real value. That is just not true. There is as much pursuit of beauty and grace in programming as there is in any other art or science—an elegant algorithm is beautiful; a tight piece of code is amazingly satisfying. There doesn't need to be any justification for that. There doesn't need to be any parallel drawn to things that have gone before.

C Quick
Reference

13

Data Types and Variables

13

All variables in C are declared or defined before they are used. A *declaration* indicates the type of a variable. If the declaration also causes storage to be set aside for the variable, it is a *definition*.

Data types in C are either *basic* or *complex* (composed of one part or many), and new types can be formed from the original types.

Declaring and Defining Variables

A variable declaration consists of a type specifier followed by the names of one or more variables of that type. Multiple variable names are separated by commas. The declarations

```
int x;
char yesno, ok;
```

declare x as a variable of type int, and yesno and ok as variables of type char.

Each variable name can be followed by an optional initialization expression:

```
int ordered = 1, onhand = 0;
float total = 43.132;
```

The variables ordered and onhand are initialized to values of 1 and 0, respectively, and total is initialized to 43.132.

Pointers can be initialized to the constant value NULL or 0.

Basic Data Types

Table 13.1 gives the basic data types for C, their ranges, and their sizes. The char, int, short, and long types may be either signed or unsigned (values start at 0).

Table 13.1. C data types, ranges, and sizes.

Type (Bits)	Range	Size in Bytes
char (signed)	−128 to +127	1 (8)
char (unsigned)	0 to +255	1 (8)
enum	−32,768 to+32,767	2 (16)
int (signed)	−32,768 to +32,767	2 (16)
char (unsigned)	0 to +65,535	2 (16)
short (signed)	−32,768 to +32,767	2 (16)
short (unsigned)	0 to +65,535	2 (16)
long (signed)	−2,147,483,648 to +2,147,483,647	4 (32)
long (unsigned)	0 to +4,294,967,295	4 (32)
float	3.4E−38 to 3.4E+38	4 (32)
double	1.7E−308 to 1.7E+308	8 (64)
long double	1.7E−308 to 1.7E+308	8 (64)
pointer (near, _cs, _ds, _es, _ss pointers)		2 (16)
pointer (far, huge pointers)		4 (32)

char

The char type is used to represent characters or integral values in a limited range (−128 to 127 or 0 to 255). Constants of type char can be characters enclosed in single quotation marks ('A','x'). Nonprinting characters (tab, formfeed, etc.) can be represented conveniently with escape sequences ('\t','\f'). For example:

```
char fstline;
static char drive = 'B';
```

13

The backslash (\) introduces an escape sequence. The standard escape sequences are listed in Table 13.2. Note that the escape sequence for a single backslash is a double backslash (\\).

Table 13.2. Escape sequences.

Character	Meaning
\a	Alert (bell) character
\b	Backspace
\f	Formfeed
\n	Newline (carriage return and line feed pair)
\r	Carriage return
\t	Tab (horizontal)
\v	Tab (vertical)
\\	Backslash
\?	Question mark
\'	Single quotation mark
\"	Double quotation mark
\nnn	Octal number
\xnn	Hexadecimal number
'\0'	Null character (string terminator)

To support C programming on terminals that lack certain characters, such as braces ({}) and brackets ([]), the ANSI C Draft Standard establishes the use of trigraphs. Trigraphs consist of two question marks with a third punctuation character, as shown in Table 13.3.

Table 13.3. Trigraph sequences.

Trigraph	Equals
??(	[
??)	]

Trigraph	Equals
??<	{
??>	}
??/	\
??'	^
??-	~
??=	#
??!	¦

int, short, and long

These types represent integers (whole numbers) in C. The short and int types are the same in all microcomputer implementations of C. They provide a means of specifying a more exact size or range on certain computers. The size of an int can vary from computer to computer, but the sizes of short and long are guaranteed. A short will be two bytes and a long will be four bytes. If you are writing programs to be used on different computers, use short and long instead of int.

Constants for integers can be

◆ Decimal, such as 3, 111, or 43859876

◆ Octal, which are prefixed by 0, as in 012 (= 10 decimal) or 076 (= 62 decimal)

◆ Hexadecimal, which are prefixed by 0x or 0X, such as 0x12 (= 18 decimal) or 0x2f (= 47 decimal)

Long integer constants use I or L as a suffix: 012L or 0x12L. The suffix U may be used by some compilers (Turbo C, for example) to indicate an unsigned constant. Integers can be declared and initialized, as in these examples:

```
int noOfBooks;
static short noOfPages;
static short nameLength = strlen(yourName);
long recsUsed = 832198;
```

13

float and *double*

The float and double types apply to decimal numbers. The float type has at least 6 digits of precision (that is, at least 6 significant digits), while the double type has at least 10 significant digits. The IEEE floating point standard, followed by most C compilers, specifies 15 digits of precision for doubles and 18 digits of precision for long doubles.

Examples of floating point constants include the following:

3.14159

1.3E–75

–812.92

Examples of floating point variables include the following:

```
float aveTime;
static float distance=483.71;
double lightyears=56.3819c7;
```

enum

The enum type is an "ordered list" of items as integer constants. This new type from the ANSI standard can be especially useful for comparisons and can be used in place of #define statements. Unless specified otherwise, the first member of an enumerated set of values has the value of 0, but you can also specify values. The declaration

```
enum weekdays {Sunday, Monday, Tuesday, Wednesday,
    Thursday, Friday, Saturday}
```

means that Sunday = 0, Monday = 1, etc. However, if you use

```
enum weekdays {Sunday, Monday, Tuesday = 10, Wednesday,
    Thursday, Friday, Saturday}
```

then Sunday still equals 0, and Monday still equals 1; but now Tuesday equals 10, Wednesday equals 11, etc. This is a much easier way to define several variables and can be used in most cases where #define statements, such as #define SUNDAY 0, were used in the past.

An enumerated type can be used to declare a variable

```
enum weekdays anyday;
```

then used with

```
anyday = Tuesday;
```

or with

```
anyday = Saturday;
if (anyday >= Friday)
    printf("Today must be %d\n", anyday);
```

then the value "Saturday" will *not* be printed. Instead, the value 6 (if Sunday=0, etc.) will be displayed. In order to get the string "Saturday" to print, you would also have to establish an array such as

```
char daynames[][9] = {"Sunday", "Monday", "Tuesday",
    "Wednesday", "Thursday", "Friday", "Saturday"};
```

and use the statement

```
if (anyday >= Friday)
    printf("Today must be %s\n", daynames[anyday]);
```

to obtain

```
"Today must be Saturday"
```

Pointers

The *pointer* is a special data type that holds the address of another variable. A pointer is declared by using the asterisk (*) in front of a variable name, as in

```
float *wirelength;
char *index;
```

A pointer can be initialized or assigned the address of a variable by using the address operator (&) before the variable name:

```
wirelength = &wire2;
```

The *indirection operator* (also an asterisk) is used to access the value in the address contained in a pointer. For example,

```
*wirelength = 30.5;
```

means "assign the value 30.5 to the float variable pointed to by wirelength." Because wirelength contains the address of wire2, this statement has the same effect as

```
wire2 = 30.5;
```

See the section "Type Qualifiers" and "Memory Models" for more information on near, far, and huge pointers. See the section "Operators and Expressions" for further discussion of the * and & operators.

Variables in C have lvalues and rvalues. An lvalue, or left value, is the address of the variable. An rvalue, or right value, is the content of the variable. In other words, a pointer is used to get the rvalue of a variable by using the indirection operator.

Initializing Pointers

Pointers must be initialized by assigning an address. If your program assigns a value to a pointer (with the indirection operator *) before the pointer is initialized to an address, you risk putting data on top of other data in memory. This is called an *uninitialized pointer* and should always be assigned an address first. For example, the declaration

```
int *intptr = 847; /* WRONG */
```

stores the value 847 at the memory location whose address is found in the integer pointer intptr. That address is undefined because intptr has not yet been assigned an address.

The example, as well as any pointer, can be initialized by following these steps:

1. Use a memory-allocation function such as malloc or calloc to create storage for a pointer. For example:

```
intptr = (int *)malloc
    (sizeof(int));
```

2. Assign the pointer to an existing variable's address with the & (address) operator. For example:

```
int funcresult;
intptr = &funcresult;
```

Another "workaround" is not to use a pointer variable at all but to apply the & (address) operator to the variable directly when an address is required. This is the case in the following function, which needs a pointer as a parameter:

```
int intparam;            /* declare an integer
                            variable*/
int result;              /* holds the function
                            result */
int calcdiff(int *fstvar);  /* function prototype */

result = calcdiff(&intparam);
```

Pointers to strings are initialized by assigning the string to the pointer variable. If a string pointer is declared as char *strptr;, then the following assigns the string to the pointer:

```
strptr = "Enter a whole number:   ";
```

Pointers to Values

To use a pointer to point to a value, use the indirection operator (*) in front of the pointer variable to assign a value to what the pointer addresses:

```
double *total;
*total = 3489.391;
```

or use alternatively the address operator (&) to assign the pointer to the variable address:

```
double *total;
double calctotal;
total = &calctotal;
```

Pointers and Arrays

Working with array subscripts is part of the power of pointers. If a program declares

```
float *arraypointer;
float floatarray[30]);
```

then arraypointer can be assigned the address of the beginning (the first element) of floatarray by using

```
arraypointer = floatarray;
```

13

or

```
arraypointer = &floatarray[0];
```

No & (address operator) is needed when using the array name because compilers evaluate the name as an address automatically. However, the address operator is required when referring to an individual element in an array.

The name `floatarray[3]` also could be written as `*(floatarray + 3)` because the compiler converts it to this form. (Note the generic form of the term would be `**(arrayname + i)`, where `i` is the value of the array element desired.)

Pointers can be treated like arrays, so they may have subscripts. `arraypointer[2]` is the same as `*(arraypointer + 2)`.

Note: There is a difference between using pointers and arrays. Pointers are variables and can be incremented and decremented (for example, `++arraypointer`). This cannot be done to an array because the array name is a constant address (for example, `floatarray++` is illegal). Take care not to go past the upper and lower limits of the array.

When using pointers to move within arrays, the pointer does not move one byte at a time unless you are using `char` arrays. The pointer moves the size of an individual array element or whatever type is being pointed to. In the previous example of an array of `float`, the pointer will move `sizeof(float)`, or four bytes, as it is incremented or decremented. *Pointer arithmetic* involves the following:

◆ Assigning pointers of the same type.

◆ Assigning a pointer or comparing it to 0.

◆ Incrementing or decrementing a pointer.

◆ Adding, subtracting, or comparing pointers to members of an array.

♦ Relational and equality tests along with logical AND and OR.

♦ Addition or subtraction of integers.

♦ Converting from other pointer types or converting to and from integers.

Pointers to Pointers

Pointers can point to other pointers (called "*double indirection*"). Pointers often are used like this, especially with dynamic heaps where memory may be shifting to make larger areas of free memory. By using a single pointer, you would lose track of the address of the information and thus create a dangling pointer.

Double indirection would be used like this: char **fstvar makes a pointer to another character pointer. You could even have char ****strptr (a pointer to a pointer to a pointer to a char pointer).

When working with multidimensional arrays such as a two-dimensional array, a pointer to a pointer can be used to access any element in the array. Because a pointer assigned to the name of an array accesses the beginning of the array (arraypointer = floatarray;), then using *(arraypointer + 3) would access the first element of the fourth row of the array (array subscripts start with 0). To get the ith element (in this example, the sixth element) of the fourth row, you would use the expression

```
*(arraypointer + 3) + 5
```

To manipulate the contents of that location, which is equal to floatarray[3][5], use the expression

```
*(*(arraypointer + 3) + 5) = 31.185;
```

The expression char *argv[], which is an array of character pointers pointing to command-line arguments, also can be expressed using double indirection as in char **argv. A new command-line argument can be obtained by incrementing the pointer: argv++.

Pointers to Functions

Pointers can point to functions. The declaration

```
int (*ptrtofunction)(void);
```

13

creates a pointer to a function that returns an integer. This can be useful in making more generic routines or passing function names as parameters to other functions (see bsearch and qsort). Because a function name is evaluated as an address, no operator is needed when using the pointer or in making assignments. A pointer to a function is used as a parameter of another function, such as qsort. A function pointer can be assigned to another function by using its name without any parameters, as in the following:

```
ptrtofunction = calcdiff;
```

void

Void is a special type that is valueless. It has three distinct uses (also see the section "Keywords"):

1. The void type is used as a generic pointer without a type and can be used with any other type pointer. For example:

   ```
   void *dummyptr;
   ```

   Earlier versions of C usually used a character pointer as a "generic" pointer). For example:

   ```
   char *anyptr;
   ```

   A void pointer, however, cannot be "dereferenced" by using the * operator. void also can be used in casts to "relieve" an item of its type. For example, using the statement

   ```
   (void)strcpy(filename, fileinput)
   ```

   quiets the lint utility (a C program checker) by signifying that you are ignoring the return value of the function, because strcpy normally returns a character pointer.

2. The void type can be used to signify an empty parameter list. For example:

   ```
   int sumtotals(void);
   ```

3. The void type is used as the return type of a function that does not return a value. For example:

   ```
   void writedit(introw, intcol);
   ```

If your compiler does not yet support the `void` type, you can add this statement to compensate:

```
#define void;
```

This causes the compiler to ignore the term `void` and allows the use of `void` in empty function parameter lists.

Complex or Aggregate Data Types

C's complex types include *arrays*, which include "strings" or arrays of characters, *structures*, *unions*, and *bitfields*.

Arrays

An *array* is a block of consecutive data items of the same type, referenced with a subscript. All arrays in C start with the subscript `[0]`. For instance, the single-dimensional array specified in

```
int grades[30];
```

is capable of storing 30 individual grades, `grades[0]` through `grades[29]`. A two-dimensional array such as

```
float weights[10][12];
```

would allocate storage for 10 people with 12 values for each person corresponding to one per month (a total of 120 values). Other dimensions are added by adding another set of brackets `[ ]`.

In a nondefining declaration, such as in another source module or any place where no storage has been set aside by the compiler, a multidimensional array could be declared without specifying the size of the first dimension, as in

```
extern double planetDistance[][10];
```

The size is obtained by the compiler from the original declaration.

The number of elements (members) of an array can be determined by dividing the size of the entire array by the size of one of the elements, as shown in this formula:

```
noofelements =
    sizeof(arrayname) / sizeof(arrayname[0])
```

This is often specified as a #define statement.

Static and Auto Arrays

A *static array* can be initialized when it is declared with

```
static char progerr[] = "Disk door not closed.";
```

An *auto array* can be initialized only with a constant expression in ANSI C. (See the section "Storage Class Modifiers" for an explanation of static and auto arrays.) For example:

```
int smallmatrix[2][2] = {{32, 2}, {95, 70}};
```

If not all members are assigned a value, they are initialized to 0 by the compiler.

Arrays of Pointers

An array of pointers to characters can be initialized with

```
char *colors[] = {"magenta", "red",
    "mauve", "orchid","rose"};
```

and then can be used like any other array. Using the array of characters above,

```
printf("colors = %s\n", colors[3]);
```

would display

```
colors = orchid
```

Arrays of pointer allow manipulation of complex data structures by moving only the pointers rather than the data itself. See the section "Pointers and Arrays" for more information about the relationship between pointers and arrays.

Strings

Strings are simply character arrays (for example, char anystr[30]), although they often are used in connection with character pointers. Strings are always terminated with a null value ('\0') in C. No byte is set aside to hold the length; length must always be determined through a function such as strlen. String literals (constants) may extend over two lines without special punctuation, according to the ANSI standard, and will be merged together. For example:

```
char longmsg[] =    "This will be an example of a long"
                    "string for a literal.";
```

yields

```
"This will be an example of a long string for a
    literal."
```

Arrays need not always specify the size of a dimension (except the last one) because the compiler can determine size. The statement

```
char fruitnames[][10] =
    {"orange", "banana", "apple"};
```

is interpreted by the compiler as an effective declaration of

```
char fruitnames[3][10];
```

for allocating storage.

Structures

Structures (structs) are collections of data—often of different types—that can be acted upon as a whole. A structure can hold simple data types, such as characters, floats, arrays, and enumerated types. A structure also can hold types such as other structures, arrays, or unions. For example:

```
struct bookreference {
    char title[50];
    char author[30];
    int pages;
    int pubyear;
};
```

A variable could be declared by using

```
struct bookreference computerbooks;
```

To initialize and use the variable computerbooks, for example, do the following:

```
struct bookreference computerbooks =
    {"Debugging C", "Robert Ward", 349, 1986};
```

To assign a specific value to the variable, use

```
computerbooks.pages = 219;
```

Pointers to structures can also be made:

```
struct bookreference *ptrbookref;
```

which would be used when referring to member, such as

```
ptrbookref->pages = 219;
```

(see also Chapter 14, "Operators and Expressions").

Many compilers now allow structures to be passed "en masse" to functions, allow structures to be returned by functions, and may even allow an entire structure to be assigned to another structure without having to do it member-by-member. You cannot, however, compare two structures to see if they are equal.

Structures also may contain pointers to structures of the same type. In other words, this example,

```
struct bookreference
    {
    char title[50];
    char author[30];
    int pages;
    int pubyear;
    struct bookreference abook; /*ILLEGAL*/
    };
```

could not contain a member such as

```
struct bookreference abook;
```

but it *could* contain a pointer to the structure as

```
struct bookreference *bookptr;
```

These are called *self-referential structures* and can be used to build complex data structures, such as linked lists, binary trees, and so on.

13

Unions

Unions are almost identical to structures in their syntax. Unions provide a method of storing more than one type (although only one is used at any given time) at one memory location. In a union, enough storage is reserved for the largest member.

In this example, storage is set aside for four bytes (the size of a float). Only one part of a union is active at a time, and the programmer is responsible for remembering which piece is active. When using the union definition

```
union numtype {
    short anint;
    long  along;
    float afloat;
};
```

and declaring a variable with

```
union numtype numbertype;
```

the first part could be used as

```
numbertype.anint = 341;
```

or the second part could be used as

```
numbertype.along = 5882094
```

and so on. The preceding union could be initialized as:

```
union numtype { short anint; long
    along; float afloat; } = {57};
```

This form may vary and may not be supported by some compilers.

Bitfields

Bitfields often are used to put integers into spaces smaller than the compiler normally would use and are thus implementation-dependent. The compiler controls attributes such as the ordering of bits, whether unsigned or signed integers can be used, and so on. A bitfield always is specified within a structure by using a colon after the integer declaration along with the number of bits to be used (usually from 1 to 16). For example:

```
struct sample {
    int fstfield:4;
    short sndfield:6;
};
```

This sets up a member called fstfield where an integer will be fit into four bits, and a second member called sndfield where the integer will be fit into six bits.

Reading Complex Declarations

Some declarations in C can be complex and difficult to untangle. There is a fairly simple method, called the "right-left" rule, which facilitates reading by finding the innermost set of parentheses and working clockwise, starting to the right of this point. For example:

```
float (*doCalc)(double fst, double snd);
```

1. Look for a set of parentheses first. Because there are two of them here, look for one without types inside (*doCalc). The *identifier* here is doCalc.

2. Now look to the right of the identifier within the parentheses. In the example, there is nothing. If there had been something, the identifier might have been an array.

3. Look to the left of the identifier within parentheses. In the example, there is an asterisk, indicating a pointer.

4. Because the identifier is a pointer, look to the right again to find a set of parentheses holding what appear to be parameters. This indicates a pointer to a function.

5. On the left of the identifier is the term float, indicating that the pointer points to a function returning a float.

6. Look to the right of the identifier and examine what is in the parentheses. There are two parameters of type double.

You find that you are dealing with a pointer to a function that returns a float and uses two parameters of type double.

A method of simplifying such complicated declarations is by using the `typedef` modifier. The preceding example would become

```
typedef float (*doCalc)(double fst, double snd);
```

and then could be used to define other variables such as

```
doCalc aspectRatio;
```

instead of

```
float (*aspectRatio)(double fst, double snd);
```

Storage Class Modifiers

These modifiers are used to change the way a C compiler allocates storage for variables. `Extern`, `static`, and `typedef` may be used with both variables and functions.

auto

`auto` indicates that a variable is automatic or local (restricted) in scope. This means the variable comes into being within the current block and does not exist after leaving the block. `auto` is permitted only in the heads of program blocks. Because `auto` is the default modifier, it is rarely seen.

extern

`extern` indicates a variable or function that is static in scope and is declared elsewhere outside the module. This lets the linker know it should not look in this program module for the variable or function. A common example of an `extern` is when you need to share data globally between two or more files.

register

`register` tells the compiler to place (if possible) the variable into the machine registers. This modifier is used to improve a program's speed and efficiency, especially for loop-counter variables (`for`, `while`) and for pointers.

register is usually restricted for use with char and int variables and their pointers. You cannot use the & operator with register variables. Also, register normally is *not* used with parameters. It is better programming style to declare local register variables within the routine and assign the parameters to them.

static

static may modify either variables or functions. It tells the compiler that the variable or function should be kept for the duration of the program from the point of declaration—even when going into other modules. A static variable retains its previous value from one function call to another.

typedef

typedef does not really seem to fit in with the rest. It normally is used when defining variables or functions and means a new type is being formed. (Actually, you can rename only an existing type.)

typedef is underused. It allows levels of data abstraction and makes for greater program clarity. Data abstraction involves taking a "concrete" form of data, such as a stack, and putting it into a form using variables. If a variable were defined as

```
typedef struct BOOKREFERENCE;
```

then, instead of using

```
struct bookreference computerbook;
```

to declare a variable, you could use

```
BOOKREFERENCE computerbook;
```

Another example is:

```
typedef char *STRING;
```

where you then can use the following declaration:

```
STRING booktitle;
```

in place of

```
char *booktitle;
```

This at least hides the fact you are using a struct as the underlying data type. Using `typedefs` also can aid portability; only the `typedef` need be changed instead of each statement using the new type.

Type Qualifiers

Type qualifiers define additional qualities of types besides storage and describe the "stability" of a variable. They may be used by themselves or with other type specifiers.

const

`const` is a new modifier from the ANSI standard. `const` signals to the compiler that this variable's value cannot be changed during the program by things such as side effects, incrementing, and decrementing. A `const` pointer cannot be changed even though the object it points to could be changed.

Notice there is a difference between specifying

A. a variable (changing) pointer that points to a constant (nonchanging) object, such as

```
const char *pointer_to_const_char;
```

and

B. a constant (nonchanging) pointer that points to a variable (changing) object, such as

```
char *const const_pointer_to_char;
```

In A the value or address of the pointer may change, but not the value of the character it points to. In B the value or address of the pointer should *not* change, but the value of the character to which it points can change. `const` may be used by itself without a type, in which case a type of `int` is assumed.

volatile

`volatile` is the opposite of the `const` qualifier and states the variable can be changed at any time, not only by the program but

13

also by interrupts or by other outside factors—the real-time clock, for example. `volatile` also may prevent the compiler from performing any optimizations on the variable because its value can be changed so readily. `volatile` is a new ANSI modifier also.

Scope and Variable Lifetime

Variables and functions in C exist for different durations. Global variables and functions come into being at the beginning of the program and last until the end of it. Others exist only while certain sections of the program are active. The area of a program where a variable is active or visible is called the `scope` of that variable (see Table 13.4).

ANSI C defines four types of scope: *function prototype* (limited to labels for `goto` statements), *block, file,* and *function.* The variable may be visible to the entire program, to a group of source files, to a family of functions, to a single function, or to an individual block of code. (See also the section "Storage Class Modifiers.")

A variable is *defined* only once, and at that time storage is allocated to it. A variable is *declared* whenever it is referenced in another file, and no storage is set aside during a declaration. A variable is *initialized* by the compiler only once (if at all) during the program when variables are defined and allocated storage.

Complex types (`union`, `struct`, arrays) of type `auto` usually cannot be initialized by the compiler. It is good practice to initialize them yourself as insurance.

A variable should be defined in one file `char anychar` and initialized there. For example:

```
char anychar = 'k';
```

A variable can be referenced in a declaration with the word `extern` in another file (`extern char anychar`) and should not be initialized there. Arrays of type extern may have empty brackets. For example:

```
extern float beamWeights[];
```

Table 13.4. Scope of variables in C.

Variable	*Scope*
global	Global variables consist of variables defined before and outside of main(); exist from beginning to end of program; normally initialized to 0 by the compiler.
external	External variables are defined outside the current module and exist as do static variables; usually initialized to 0 by the compiler.
external static	External static variables consist of a static variable declared outside a function. It is active from that point to the end of the program. An external static variable could be put in a module containing a family of related functions to be private only to those functions. It retains its value throughout the program and is initialized to 0 by the compiler.
static	Static variables exist from definition to the end of the program and occur inside a function. They retain their values between function calls and are normally initialized to 0 by the compiler.
auto	Auto variables exist only within the block where they were defined: within a function, a loop, or inside braces. They are not initialized.
register	Register variables are the same as auto variables.

14

Operators and Expressions

14

C has a powerful set of operators. Used well, they add to the language's expressiveness and efficiency. Used poorly, they lead to expressions that are difficult to read or give the wrong result.

Table 14.1, C Operator Precedence and Associativity, lists the operators for C. The table shows the operators grouped from highest to lowest precedence. Operators within a group have the same precedence and associativity.

Table 14.1. C operator precedence and associativity.

Operator	Function	Assoc. *	Example
( )	membership	L	`total = intsum(cost, tax);`
[ ]	membership	L	`midtermgrade = grades[3];`
.	membership	L	`size = body.waist;`
->	membership	L	`size = bodyptr->waist;`
-	unary	R	`refund = -refundamt;`
+	unary	R	`age = +age;`
~	unary	R	`bitsoff = ~1;`
!	unary	R	`keepgoing = !done;`
*	unary	R	`filename = *fileptr;`
&	unary	R	`filenameptr = &filename;`
++	unary	R	`++loopcount;` (increment)
--	unary	R	`--countdown;` (decrement)
sizeof	unary	R	`storage = sizeof(float);`
(type)	unary	R	`avedays = (int)days/3;`

14

Operator	Function	Assoc. *	Example
*	multi.	L	`dollars = quarters * .25`
/	multi.	L	`averageage = totalyears/students;`
%	multi.	L	`remainderodd = anynumber % 2;`
+	additive	L	`newnumber = oldnumber +amount;`
-	additive	L	`totaldue = subtotal - credit;`
<<	bitwise	L	`newvalue = equipbyte << 8;`
>>	bitwise	L	`mode = monitorcheck >> 2;`
<	relational	L	`if (today < Friday);`
>	relational	L	`if (linecount > 66);`
<=	relational	L	`while (linewidth <= 80);`
>=	relational	L	`while (bottommargin >= 6);`
==	equality	L	`if (leftmargin == 10);`
!=	equality	L	`while (flag != first);`
&	bitwise	L	`bitchecked = mode & 0xFF;`
^	bitwise	L	`desiredbit = status ^ 0x80;`
¦	bitwise	L	`bitset = modecheck ¦ 0xF;`
&&	logical	L	`while (mode==edit && flag!=insert);`
¦¦	logical	L	`if (c == 'Y' ¦¦ c == 'y');`

continues

Table 14.1. continued

Operator	Function	Assoc. *	Example
?:	conditional	R	`result = mode > 0 ?` `errorvalue : okvalue;`
=, *=, /=, %=, +=, -=, <<=, >>=, &=, ^=, |=		R	`grandtotal +=` `dailyamount;`
,	series	L	`for (count=1, state=0;` `count<10; ++count);`

* L = left-to-right associativity, R = right-to-left associativity

Expressions

An *expression* is a combination of operators (such as + and =) and operands (variables) that produces a value. This means an expression can be used in most places where variables are used. Operators cause an action to be performed on the operands.

In C, no guarantee is given as to the order in which operators and operands are evaluated except in the cases of ¦¦ (logical OR), && (logical AND), ?: (ternary), and the series operator (,), which force left-to-right evaluation.

Expressions can change a variable *indirectly* during expression evaluation. An example of one of these "side effects" is a function that changes the value of a global variable when the global variable is not passed as an argument to the function.

Each operator belongs to a group that has a higher or lower *precedence* (rank of evaluation) than another group. For example, the expression

```
x * y / (sizeof(z) * 3)
```

contains five operators and four operands. The parentheses have the highest precedence, so what is inside (`sizeof(z)` `*` `3`) is evaluated first. The `sizeof` operator is used, then the result of that operation is multiplied by 3. The other multiplication and division operators are performed on the value from inside the parentheses. Not using the parentheses around `sizeof(z) * 3` would result in a different answer.

When two or more operators have the same precedence, an attribute called *associativity* takes over. Associativity is the order in which operators are grouped with operands as the expression is evaluated. This means that when two operators have the same precedence in an expression, the compiler uses the one that would come first under the rules of associativity. There are two basic rules of associativity:

1. Every operator has a *direction* associated with it, and operators within a group have the same direction. If conflicting operators in an expression have the same precedence, the expression will be evaluated in the direction (left-to-right or right-to-left) associated with the operators.

2. Operators have higher precedence when used as postfix operators than as prefix operators.

In the previous example, the multiplication and division operators have the same precedence. Both operators have left to right associativity, so `y` is grouped with the multiplication operator first, rather than with the division operator. The quantity `x * y` is evaluated, then the result divided by the quantity `(sizeof(z) * 3)`.

All operators in C are evaluated from left to right except for unary, conditional (ternary), and assignment operators, which are evaluated from right to left.

Using a simpler example:

```
intresult = subtot[1] + subtot[2] - shipping;
```

Here the brackets are evaluated first, and the compiler gets the array values for `subtot`. Because the + and - operators have equal precedence and are evaluated from left to right, the two subtotals are added together, and then the shipping amount is subtracted. This would be the same as if parentheses had been used around the addition expression. For example:

```
intresult = (subtot[1] +
    subtot[2]) - shipping;
```

In expressions using operators with right-to-left associativity, such as:

```
totalDistance = planetDistance *= noOfPlanets;
```

the operand planetDistance is grouped with the operator (*=) on its right, so (planetDistance *= noOfPlanets) is evaluated and then assigned to totalDistance. To be clearer to the reader, it could have been written as:

```
totalDistance = (planetDistance *= noOfPlanets);
```

Because expressions can be used in place of variables, statements such as the following could be used (although this is not done frequently because readability and "understandability" are reduced):

```
beginpoint = 1;
fststr = "programming";
sndstr = "programming";
intvalue == (beginpoint > 3,
    (strcmp(fststr, sndstr)
    == 0));
```

Here, the two parts of the last expression are evaluated, and then the result of the last part is assigned to intvalue. In the example, beginpoint > 3 is evaluated as either 0 or 1; and because either value is less than 3, the expression returns 0 (false). The strcmp is then done to compare fststr and sndstr; and because the result of strcmp is equal to 0, a 1 (true) is returned, and the end value of intvalue equals 1.

According to the second rule for associativity, postfix operators have a higher precedence than prefix operators. If you are using the expression

```
arrayelement = *arraypointer++;
```

the pointer is incremented before the indirection operator is applied. The result is assigned to arrayelement.

Operators

This section describes the C operators and their functions. These operators provide a rich variety of possible expressions.

Table 14.1 displays the operators in C arranged from highest to lowest precedence by group. The direction of associativity for each is indicated (L for left-to-right; R for right-to-left). The major groups of operators are membership, unary, arithmetic, bitwise shift, relational, equality, bitwise logical, logical, conditional (ternary), assignment, and series operators.

There are four general types of operators, depending on the number of operands required. *Unary operators* require one operand. *Binary operators* (arithmetic, bitwise, relational, equality, logical, assignment, and series operators) require two operands. There is only one *ternary operator*, the conditional operator, and it uses three operands. Membership operators are classified as "postfix expressions" along with the postfix increment (++) and postfix decrement (--) operators. A postfix expression means the operator occurs after the expression. See Table 14.1 for the specific operators within each type of operators.

In C, a symbol used as an operator, such as the ampersand (&), can mean more than one thing. This is called "operator overloading" and can be confusing. For instance, the ampersand may be used as the address operator (&studentscore), the bitwise AND operator (equipbyte & bytemask), or the logical AND operator ((begin == 1) && (num < 5)).

Another example is the asterisk (*), which may signify a pointer in a variable declaration, the indirection operator, or the multiplication operator.

Membership Operators

There are four *membership operators*: parentheses (), brackets [], dot (.), and arrow (->).

Membership operators in C deal with complex data types, such as functions, structures, and arrays. They can be used in conjunction with other operators like the indirection and address operators to provide complex expressions for obtaining a particular data item.

As an example, consider finding the 29th element of the 5th row in an array of doubles (studentgrade) where the element is a member of a structure (studentstruct). This structure is the 4th member of an array of structures (studentdata). The array of structures is also referenced by an array of pointers (studentno).

```c
#include <stdio.h>

void main(void)
{
  int count;                 /* loop counter */
  double grade;              /* holds final grade */
  typedef struct student     /* define structure
                                type */
    {
    char *studentname;
    double studentgrade[5][30];
  } studentstruct;

  /* define array of structures and pointers to the
     structures */
  static studentstruct studentdata[10],
        *studentno[10];

  /*  assign the pointers to array elements  */
  for (count = 0; count < 10; count++)
    studentno[count] = &studentdata[count];

  /*  assign a value to an element in the array  */
  studentdata[3].studentgrade[4][28] = 3.25;

  /*  print out 5 of the students' values using the
      pointers */
  for (count = 0; count < 5; count++)
    {
    grade = studentno[count]->studentgrade[4][28];
    printf("Student %1d has a
          grade = %1.3f\n",
          count,      grade);
    }
}
```

The output for all students other than studentno[3] is zero. The
output for studentno[3] is 3.25. Note that data can be referenced
through the pointer array rather than through the structure array
by using the "arrow" operator and subscripts.

Specific information about the four membership operators is
given in Table 14.2.

Table 14.2. Membership operators.

Operator	Name	Description
( )	Parentheses	Parentheses are used in functions calls and contain parameters used by the function or the keyword void if no parameters are used. For example: `strcat(filename, fileext);`
[ ]	Brackets	Brackets are used as subscripts in arrays (and sometimes in pointers) to indicate an individual array element. For example, the following expression refers to the second element in the fourth row of the array: `studentScores[3][1]`
.0	Dot	The dot operator allows access to a "field" or structure member as in: `fileinfo.filename = inputfilename;`
->	Arrow	The "arrow" operator (a hyphen and greater than sign combined) is used when referring to a structure member or "field" when using a pointer to a structure. This operator can be used only with a pointer as the left operand. For example: `fileptr->filename = inputfilename;`

continues

Table 14.2. continued

Operator	Name	Description
		Another way to refer to a structure member is to use parentheses and the * (indirection) operator along with the dot operator:
		`*(fileptr).filename = inputfilename;`
		Parentheses are required because the dot has higher precedence than the * operator.

Unary Operators

The unary operators are those requiring only one operand and have a high level of precedence. Table 14.3 lists the unary operators.

Table 14.3. Unary operators.

Operator	Name	Description
-	Unary Minus	The unary minus operator finds the negative value of its operand. The expression `refund = -refundamt;` assigns to `refund` the negative value of `refundamt` if it is positive. Unsigned operands produce unsigned results. The minus operator does not cause any change in the order of an expression's evaluation.

Operator	Name	Description
+	Unary Plus	The unary plus operator returns the value of the operand. It also can be used to force the order of evaluation in an expression by telling the compiler not to rearrange the order of the expression to the right of the unary plus operator. This makes it act somewhat like a set of parentheses. The unary plus is a new operator in the ANSI standard.
~	One's	The one's complement operator, the Complement tilde (~), means all bits within the affected variable (byte) are inverted: 0's become 1's, and 1's become 0's.
!	Unary	The unary (logical) negation operator, performs logical negation on its operand, so the result is 1 if the operand has a value of 0, and 0 if the operand has a value of 1. For example: `keepgoing = !done;`.
*	Pointer	The pointer indirection operator Indirection provides a means of retrieving the value pointed to by a pointer. In other words, if `anystr` is a pointer to a string, and `picturename = *anystr;`

continues

201

Table 14.3. continued

Operator	Name	Description
		then `picturename` equals "Mona Lisa" if `anystr` pointed to a string variable containing that value. Alternatively, if you use `*anystr = "Mona Lisa";` you tell the compiler to assign the value "Mona Lisa" to the variable pointed to by `anystr`.
&	Address	The address operator obtains the address of a variable or function. For example, if `anystr = &pictstruct.picturetitle;` then `anystr` will contain the address of the variable `picturetitle` within the structure `pictstruct` after execution. It is used in connection with pointers when they must be assigned to an address. The address operator may be applied also to a variable passed as a function parameter when the function is expecting to receive a pointer.
++ --	Increment Decrement	The increment operator is used to increase the value of variables, and the decrement operator is used to decrease the value of variables. They can be used either in front of (prefix) or behind (postfix) variables to give slightly different results. More information about using

Operator	Name	Description
		these operators is presented later in this section.

sizeof	Sizeof	The `sizeof` operator is not a function but an actual operator in the C language. It returns the system size of an item:
		
		`sizeof(result)`
		
		If `result` is of type `integer`, the expression normally would return 2, and
		
		`sizeof(fileptr->filename)`
		
		where
		
		`filename = "OUT.TXT"`
		
		would return 7. Using `sizeof` on a normal `near` pointer results in 2 on most systems. You can use `sizeof` to get the size of entire complex types, such as structures and unions.

(type)	Casts	Cast operators transform variables or function results from one type to another. A cast is indicated by placing the desired type inside parentheses in front of the variable or function to be changed. For more information, see the section titled "Casts."

Increment and Decrement Operators Used with Variables

Given an integer variable count equal to 1, the expression ++count means that count is incremented before being used (it is now 2) and then is used as in:

```
total += ++count;
```

If `total = 0` and `count = 1` before this statement, `count` is first incremented, then added to `total`; so `total = 2`, and `count = 2` after execution. On the other hand,

```
total += count++;
```

has a different result. `count++` means the value of `count` is used, then incremented. If `total = 0` and `count = 1` before this statement, `count` is added to `total`, then incremented; so `total = 1`, and `count = 2` after execution.

The same holds true for the decrement operator. Using `--count` means that if `count = 2` before the statement, it would equal 1 before being used. In contrast, `count--` means if `count = 2` before the statement, it is used with the value of 2, and then decremented to 1 after the statement is executed.

Increment and Decrement Operators Used with Pointers

In the case of pointers, the increment and decrement operators work differently. Pointers are not necessarily increased by a value of 1 but rather by the size of the type pointed to by the pointer.

For instance, if the pointer variable `intptr` points to an integer stored at address 1000, then after executing `++intptr`, the variable would point to address 1002, because an integer consists of 2 bytes. Additionally, if a pointer points to a structure with a size of 415 bytes (at address 1000), then that pointer will be incremented by 415 bytes to address 1415.

If the pointer points to a float, as in `*(floatptr + 3) = 0.82;`, adding a value to the pointer means adding the size of 3 floats (12 bytes) to `floatptr` and not adding 3 bytes to `floatptr`. The general form is

```
pointer +/- (n * sizeof(what the pointer points to))
```

where the compiler adds or subtracts the quantity of n number of items multiplied by the size of the item's type.

Casts

Casts transform variables or function results from one type to another. A cast is indicated by placing the desired type inside parentheses in front of the variable or function to be changed. To see why this is used, consider the following statements:

```
float total;
float noofdays;
int grandtotal;
grandtotal = total/noofdays;
```

In this sequence, you are trying to put a `float` into an integer variable, and you get a compiler error. If you add a cast,

```
grandtotal = (int)total/noofdays;
```

this would solve the problem because the compiler is now told to convert the division result into an integer.

In another example, you could convert a variable into a type required by a function parameter for proper manipulation or as a return value. If you use the function

```
int wholeNoSum(int fstvalue, int sndvalue)
```

with the following example:

```
double subtotal1, subtotal2;
int result;
result = wholeNoSum((int)
    subtotal1, (int)subtotal2);
```

you must cast the parameters as integers so that they will be properly accepted by the function.

Arithmetic Operators

The arithmetic operators (`*`, `/`, `%`, `+`, and `-`) are *binary* operators and operate as in normal arithmetic expressions. The multiplicative operators (`*`, `/`, `%`) have higher precedence than the additive operators (`+` and `-`). Table 14.4 shows the arithmetic operators.

Table 14.4. Arithmetic operators.

Operator	Name	Description
*	Multiplication	The multiplication operator multiplies two operands: `sum = value1 * value2;`
/	Division	The division operator produces the quotient of two operands: `result = value1 / value2`

%	Modulus	The modulus (remainder) operator returns the remainder of a division. If `value1` equals 12 and `value2` equals 5, then
		`result = value1 % value2;`
		puts the value of 2 into `result` (12 divided by 5 equals 2 plus a remainder of 2). A check can be made for "even" division (no remainder) by
		`if ((result = value1 % value2) == 0)`

+	Addition	The addition operator adds two operands.
-	Subtraction	The subtraction operator subtracts one operand from another.

Bitwise Operators

C provides many low-level functions to access hardware, and bit operators are part of this capability. Bit operators, which are usually binary operators, can be used only with characters or integers and consist of & (AND), ¦ (OR), ^ (XOR or exclusive OR), << (left shift) and >> (right shift). The one's complement operator (~) has been discussed previously under unary operators but is also considered a bitwise operator.

As you can see from Table 14.5, binary operators vary in precedence. The one's complement operator comes first, followed by the left and right shifts, the bitwise AND, the bitwise OR, and the bitwise exclusive OR.

Table 14.5. Bitwise operators.

Operator	Name	Description

<<	Left Shift	The left shift and right shift >> Right Shift operators function to move the bits in a byte a specified number of places. The syntax of the statement is:
		
		`variable = variable << or >> number of places;`
		
		Thus,
		
		`monitorstatus = equipbyte << 4;`
		
		would shift the bits within `equipbyte` 4 places to the left and place the result into `monitorstatus`. Shift operators are often useful when performing hardware-related tasks, such as checking equipment status and port values.

&	Bitwise AND	The bitwise AND operator returns a bit value of 1 if both bits it compares have values of 1; otherwise, it returns a value of 0.
¦	Bitwise OR	The bitwise inclusive OR operator returns a value of 1 if either bit it compares has a value of 1, it returns a 1; otherwise, it returns a 0.

continues

14

Table 14.5. continued

Operator	Name	Description
^	Bitwise XOR	The bitwise exclusive OR operator (XOR) returns a value of 0 unless one bit has a value of 1 and the other bit compared has a value of 0.

Another use of the shift operators is for dividing or multiplying values by powers of 2 because the shift operators are more efficient than using the division and multiplication operators. This means that shifting an integer, such as 17, to the left by 3, is the same as 17 x 8 = 136.

Relational Operators

The *relational operators* are used to compare two values. They are <, >, <=, and >=. The relational operators return either 0 (false) or 1 (true). Even pointers of the same type can be compared, but not complex types, such as entire structures, unions, or arrays although one member or element can be compared to another individual member or element. Table 14.6 shows the relational operators.

Table 14.6. Relational operators.

Operator	Name	Description
<	Less than	The less than operator compares two values and returns a value of 1 if the first operand has a value less than that of the second operand; otherwise, 0 is returned.
>	Greater than	The greater than operator compares two values and returns a value of 1 if the first operand

Operator	Name	Description
		has a value greater than that of the second operand; otherwise, 0 is returned.
<=	Less than or equal to	The less than or equal to operator compares two values and returns a value of 1 if the first operand has a value less than or equal to that of the second operand; otherwise, 0 is returned.
=>	Greater than or equal to	The greater than or equal to operator compares two values and returns a value of 1 if the first operand has a value greater than or equal to that of the second operand; otherwise, 0 is returned.

Equality Operators

The equality operators are == and != in C and stand for "is equal to" and "is not equal to," respectively. They require two operands and return either 0 (false) or 1 (true). Both operators are used to examine the relationships of its operands. Table 14.7 contains more information on the equality operators.

Table 14.7. Equality operators.

Operator	Name	Description
==	Is equal to	The "is equal to" operator returns a value of 1 if the expression is true; otherwise, 0 is returned. If x = 3, then the expression (x == 3) is true. If, however, x = 93, then the test (x == 3) is false.

continues

Table 14.7. continued

Operator	Name	Description
!=	Is not equal to	The "is not equal to" operator tests both its operands to see if the first is not equal to the second and returns 1 if it is true, or 0 if false.

Note the difference between the = and == operators. The = operator provides assignment; the == operator tests equality. If the variable starttime = 1 and the variable begintime = 2 exist, then using the statement:

```
if (starttime = begintime)
    printf("Time to start\n");
```

means the value of begintime is assigned to starttime, so starttime now equals 2. The compiler sees this as "if (2)...", so the program prints "Time to start" because the if statement was true (not 0). If the expression were written:

```
if (starttime == begintime)
    printf("Time to start\n");
```

then the compiler first checks to see if the values of starttime and begintime are equal. starttime = 1, and begintime = 2, so they are not equal. The compiler, therefore, continues the same as if it were "if (0)...", and the statement "Time to start" is not printed. Both forms of the if statement are legal in C, so you must be careful to check this.

Logical Operators

Logical operators compare two expressions and return a value of 0 (false) or 1 (true). The logical AND has precedence over the logical OR. Logical operators are often used in if...else statements or loops where conditional expressions are allowed. See Table 14.8 for more information on the logical operators.

C allows the logical expressions to "short circuit." In other words, when using the expression:

```
if (c == 'Y' || c == 'y')
```

if c has the value of 'Y' (making the expression true), then the second part of the expression (c == 'y') is not evaluated.

Table 14.8. Logical operators.

Operator	Name	Description
&&	Logical AND	The logical AND operator returns 0 and does not evaluate the second part if the expression to the left of the operator is false; otherwise; 1 is returned.
||	Logical OR	The logical OR operator returns 1 and does not evaluate the second part if the expression to the left of the operator is true; otherwise, 0 is returned.

Conditional (Ternary) Operator

The conditional (or *ternary*) operator consists of the question mark and colon used together and requires three operands. It substitutes an if...else clause in many ways and could result in more efficient code from the compiler. The following statement:

```
result = mode > 0 ? errorvalue : okvalue;
```

is read as:

```
if mode > 0 then result = errorvalue
    else result = okvalue.
```

The conditional operator could also be used in a function return statement such as

```
return(mode == finished ? 0 : 1);
```

which is read as

```
if (mode == finished) then return(0)
    else return;
```

and causes 0 to be returned by the function if mode == finished; otherwise, 1 is returned.

Assignment Operators

The *assignment operators* are binary and are combinations of operators and the equal sign (=) used to shorten expressions. For example, the expression

```
grandtotal = grandtotal + dailyamount;
```

repeats the variable grandtotal. C allows you to use the expression

```
grandtotal += dailyamount;
```

which means the same thing without repeating the second grandtotal. Simple assignment is provided by using the equal sign alone, and complex assignment is provided by using the equal sign combined with another operator. The assignment operators are given in Table 14.9.

Table 14.9. Assignment operators.

Operator	Description
=	The equal sign provides simple assignment of a value to the operand on the left of the = operator, so to assign the value of 3.14159 to a float, use pivalue = 3.14159;.
*=	The multiplication symbol and equal sign are used to express multiplying the left-hand operand by the right-hand operand and assigning the result back to the left-hand operand.
/=	The division symbol and equal sign are used to divide the left-hand operand by the right-hand operand and assign the resulting value to the operand on the left of the /= operator.

Operator	Description
%=	The percent sign and equal sign make this binary assignment operator. The left-hand operand undergoes a modulus operation with the operand to the right of the %= operator, and the remainder is assigned back to the left-hand operand.
+=	The plus and equal signs form this operator. It assigns the resulting value to the left-hand operand after first adding the left-hand and right-hand operands together.
-=	The minus and equal signs form this operator. It assigns the resulting value to the left-hand operand after first subtracting the right-hand from the left-hand operand.
<<=	This operator consists of the left shift and equal operators. The left-hand operand is shifted to the left by the amount specified in the right-hand operand, and the result is assigned back to the operand on the left. For example: `byteval <<= 4;` byteval is shifted left 4 places, then the new value is assigned to byteval.
>>=	This operator consists of the right shift and equal operators. The left-hand operand is shifted to the right by the amount specified in the right-hand operand, and the result is assigned back to the operand on the left.
&=	The &= assignment operator provides a bitwise AND of the left-hand and right-hand operands and assigns the result to the left-hand operand.
^=	The ^= assignment operator provides a bitwise exclusive OR (XOR) of the left-hand and right-hand operands and assigns the result to the left-hand operand.

continues

Table 14.9. continued

Operator	Description
¦=	The ¦= assignment operator provides a bitwise inclusive OR of the left-hand and right-hand operands and assigns the result to the left-hand operand.

Series Operator

The *series operator*, the comma, indicates a series of statements executed from left to right. It commonly is used in loops, particularly for statements. For example:

```
for (count = 1; count < 10; ++count, ++linesperpage);
```

would cause not only the variable count to be incremented each time the loop is executed but also the variable linesperpage.

Data Type Conversion

Using operators, particularly casts or arithmetic operators, can cause changes in precision of values during data conversion. Some precision may be lost during conversion from larger to smaller data types, such as from double to char, because you can lose high-order bytes. Converting from a smaller to a larger type, such as from char to float, generally preserves both the precision and the sign of the values. Table 14.10 shows the result of common type conversion operations.

Table 14.10. Data type conversions.

Original type	Converts to	Result
int, long	char	Uses low-order byte out of two
float, double*	char	float or double becomes a long, then low-order byte is used

Original type	Converts to	Result
long	int	Two bytes (low-order) used
float, double*	int	float becomes long, then least-significant two bytes are used
float, double*	long	Integer portion is taken; not defined if too long to fit into long type

Conversion within expressions using numeric types follows certain rules as stated in Table 14.11.

Table 14.11. Numeric data type conversions.

Original type	Converts to	Result
char	short	int
enum	int int	sign remains same
double	double	double
long	long long	sign remains same
unsigned	int	long unsigned long
unsigned	unsigned	unsigned
int	int	int

15

The C Processor

The C preprocessor substitutes text, merges or pastes tokens, performs a conditional compilation, includes other files as part of the source, and signals compiler directives in the source code before being handed over to the compiler.

Substitutions may be in the form of a *macro*, in which a name is assigned to a value (in a macro's simplest form); the name can then be used throughout the program. The value can be changed in the #define statement without having to change it each time the name appears in the source. In another form, a macro can be the body of a function. If parameters are used, the compiler allows any data type to be used, so routines, such as sorting and comparing, can become generic. Macros free the programmer from writing separate routines for integers, strings, and so on. ANSI C also sets up predefined macros.

Another major task of the preprocessor is to allow conditional compilation. This means certain sections of code are actually compiled or ignored, depending on whether conditions are true or false. This increases portability. Code for different environments or operating systems can be put into one source file and then compiled more than once with certain variables (conditions) set to true. The source could even be successfully compiled by different compilers if written accurately.

The preprocessor usually can be run separately from the compiler. The output from it can be directed to a file or to the screen in order to view exactly what substitutions are taking place, which #define values are active, and so on.

Predefined Macros

ANSI C requires five macros in compatible implementations. All of them start and end with two underscores, so the macro has four underscores in all.

_ _LINE_ _   The line number of the source file currently being processed, with the first line starting with 1. It is useful in error messages such as
Compilation error occurring at line 15.

__FILE__   The name of the source file currently being processed. It may encompass #include files and can be useful in error messages: Error during compilation in file c:\data\accounts.dat.

__DATE__   Contains the date that processing began on the source file in the form of mmm dd yyyy—for example, Feb 21 1988

__TIME__   A string containing the time processing began on the source file with a syntax of hh:mm:ss—for example, 10:23:14

__STDC__   A macro that is true (value of 1) if compiler conditions are set to denote ANSI C compatibility; otherwise, it is undefined

Compilers used on 8088/86 machines usually have a number of other (non-ANSI) system- or compiler-specific, predefined macros:

__PASCAL__   The same as a command-line option signaling Pascal conventions for identifiers and function parameters

__MSDOS__   Has the value of 1 for all compiles to denote the MS-DOS operating system

__CDECL__   Denotes C calling conventions are used instead of Pascal—usually the default condition

LINT_ARGS   Tells the compiler to use strong type-checking on functions (prototyping). Normally, two sets of function declarations are present in the header files, one with parameter types given to be used when LINT_ARG is defined, the other without

M_I86   This macro is always defined and tells the compiler the machine is in the 80 x 86 family of processors

Some of the above macros are not supported on some compilers.

Null Directive

The null statement or directive does not cause any action to be performed. It can act as a "filler." An example of this usage would be to replace the body of a for loop when all of the action is specified by the three expressions governing conditions. For example:

```
for (count = 1; wordlength <endvalue; count++)
}
```

This example increments count for later usage and does nothing else.

Command

The ## command creates the effect of "token pasting" in C. If the following is used:

```
#define STRING(a)    string ## a
STRING(1) = strcat(STRING(2),
    STRING(3));
```

the preprocessor merges or combines the token into

```
string1 = strcat(string2, string3);
```

White space (tabs, spaces, etc.) around the ## command is ignored.

#define Statements

#define statements are common in C and tell the compiler to substitute values for names during compilation. These statements have the general form:

```
#define <NAME> <substitution>
```

where NAME is usually in uppercase. The substitution may be a single value or something as elaborate as the entire body to a function. An example is

```
#define BLACK 0
```

or

```
#define QC "QuickC"
```

Any time the term BLACK is found by the preprocessor or compiler, the value 0 is substituted. Likewise, whenever QC is found, "QuickC"—double quotation marks and all—is substituted. If a semicolon is placed after the statement, it also will be included (probably in error). If the #define value must be carried over to another line, then the backslash (\) character should be the last thing on the line to let the compiler know a continuation will occur.

Entire functions can be turned into macros. This permits them to be truly generic because any argument can be used with them as long as the function contains the proper statements. Some compilers may put limits on the size of function macro or on the number of parameters allowed. For example:

```
#define DOCALC(a,b)
((a * b) + (a - 3) - \
(MAXINT - 71b))
```

could use integers (short, long, unsigned, etc.), floats, or doubles successfully. It would be used like this:

```
float fstfloat = 3.4
float sndfloat = 92.17
docalc(fstfloat, sndfloat);
```

and be used in place of a regular function call.

#undef Statement

Tokens may be undefined by using #undef <NAME> as in #undef BLACK. This causes the compiler to act as if the token does not exist. The term may be redefined later in the source if desired.

#include Statement

When more than one source file or header file is required by a program, the additional files can be incorporated into the source module via the #include statement. It consists of

```
#include <filename>
```

where filename may or may not require the complete path to the file, for example, #include <math.h>. Usually, the compiler allows the user to set up certain standard directories where the system header files and libraries are located and where the path is not needed. These files are enclosed in angle brackets (<>). Files not found in these standard directories are enclosed in quotation marks, and the compiler typically searches first the current default directory for these files unless a path is cited.

15 Conditional Compilation

Conditional compilation allows certain sections of code to be compiled or executed depending on conditions stated in the code. For example, code may not be compiled if a particular memory model is used or if a value is undefined.

#if, *#ifdef*, *#ifndef, #endif, #else*, and *#elif* Directives

This family of directives tells the compiler to process only certain portions of code where conditions are true. They are used basically the same as if-then-else statements. They assist in portability and working under varied conditions. The #if family also can be nested and is used with the #define statements for setting conditions.

```
#if EGA
    printf("EGA is being used.\n");
#else
    printf("Graphics hardware unknown.\n");
#endif
```

would print the first portion ("EGA is being used.") if EGA does not equal 0; otherwise, the second statement is printed. #ifdef works the same way, executing the appropriate statements when the term has been defined with #define.

#elif is a new statement from ANSI C and is like a combination #else and #if statement. #elif simplifies nesting when many levels are used. Instead of writing

```
#if condition1
    statement1;
#else
#if condition2
    statement2;
#else
    default;
#endif
#endif
```

the programmer can write

```
#if condition1
    statement1;
#elif condition2
    statement2;
#else
    default;
#endif
```

#ifdef and *#ifndef* Statements

These statements allow testing within the preprocessor to see if a name has been defined. They also can ensure that a macro is defined if not done previously so that it cannot be overlooked. Using #ifdef VAX would be valid if the statement #define VAX 1 preceded the #ifdef statement and is equivalent to #if VAX. Similarly, #ifndef checks if a name has *not* been defined.

#if defined(name) Statement

This is not implemented by all compilers but is part of ANSI C, and the defined section is actually an operator. Using

```
#if defined(MSDOS)
```

is the same as using

```
#ifdef MSDOS
```

The major advantage is in allowing more complex expressions using #if:

```
#if defined(MSDOS) && defined(ANSIC)
    printf("Now using ANSI C under MSDOS\n");
#endif
```

rather than

```
#ifdef MSDOS
#ifdef ANSIC
    printf("Now using ANSI C under MSDOS\n");
#endif
#endif
```

16

C

Memory Models and Memory Management

Microcomputers that use the 8088 family of processors let programmers choose among different memory models to make their code more efficient. This chapter discusses the different models and how to use them.

Segments

Personal computers with 8088/86/186/286 processors have a *segmented architecture*. This means their memory is not manipulated in one chunk but is divided into 64K segments. Segments start on paragraph boundaries (even multiples of 16). Addresses within a segment start at 0 hex and go to FFFF hex.

If you wish to find a particular address within one of the segments (held in 16 bits), you must specify an offset (also held in 16 bits) after the segment in the form of segment:offset. This usually is done in a 16-bit value (a pointer of 2 bytes), but some pointers can also be 32 bits (4 bytes). In reality, the absolute address is calculated by shifting the segment address left by 4 bits and then adding the offset address. This calculation yields a 20-bit address value.

Registers

A segment address is loaded into the segment register and can be used by the program. *Registers* are hardware locations that hold and manipulate values. However, if you wish to gain access to a memory location outside of this segment, you must either load that segment's address into the register or get at it by using a 32-bit value. This address is calculated by shifting the segment address value left by 16 bits and then adding the offset.

There are four registers regularly used by the program, and many microcomputer compilers use modifiers in connection with them. Modifiers include the code segment for storing code (_cs), the data segment for storing program data (_ds), the stack segment for function parameters and other information (_ss), and an extra segment (_es).

Pointers

A far pointer is a 32-bit pointer that can access memory outside of the segment currently being used. It allows programs larger than 64K (the size of one segment) or data occupying more than 64K.

A near pointer is only 16 bits (2 bytes) and accesses memory only within the current segment. It is the default pointer used by C.

There is yet another kind of pointer, the huge pointer, which is similar to the far pointer in size (32 bits), but is not subject to some problems that can occur with far pointers. The address of a huge pointer can be formed by calculating the 20-bit address value, then using the leftmost 16 bits for the segment address value and the rightmost 4 bits for the offset.

The huge pointer has the same value or address after shifting and wraps around the value when you reach the top end of the register. For example, if the huge pointer is at 714D:0000, decrementing the pointer would shift it to 714C:000F. Likewise, a huge pointer at 714C:000F would hold the address 714D:0000 when incremented.

The huge pointer has a unique address different from all other huge pointers, so any confusion is eliminated. On the other hand, huge pointers are slower in operation because they require additional math to calculate the address values.

Memory Models

C compilers on 8086-family machines support different memory models. The compilers may restrict the size of a single data item, such as an array, in the large and huge models. Usually, as in the large model, the data item cannot be larger than 64K. In the huge model, however, the data item may be larger than 64K under certain circumstances, such as a requirement that no single element be larger than 64K.

Use caution when you work with pointers and array addressing.

The C language states that the sizeof operator returns its calculated value as an integer, but you need to work with long int values with a 64K data item. Conversions such as casts must be done to correct this.

Conversions may vary from compiler to compiler. Table 16.1 shows the memory models and lists segments, code and data sizes, and pointers for each. (Key to segments: DS = Data Segment; CS = Code Segment; SS = Stack Segment; ES = Extra Segment.)

Table 16.1. Memory models for C compilers.

Memory Model	Segments	Data Pointers	Code Pointers
Small	DS, SS, ES at same address CS at different address (64K data and 64K code)	near	near
Medium	DS, SS, ES at same address CS at different address (64K data, up to 1M for code)	near	far
Compact	DS separate from SS and ES CS at different address (up to 1M for data, 64K code)	far	near
Large	CS and DS at different addresses as are SS and ES (1M each for data and code) single data item must be <64K	far	far
Huge	CS and DS at different addresses as are SS and ES (1M each for data and code) single data item can be >64K	far	far

To choose one of the various memory models, you need to know the approximate amount of storage required for your code and data. From this information you can choose the appropriate memory model. You can mix and match memory models by using one for the majority of your program (code and data), and then use the near, far, or huge modifiers with data objects or functions to access memory outside of the memory model in effect.

The special segment modifiers, which are near pointers, also come into play here. For example,

```
int _ds *anyptr;
```

creates a pointer to type int into the data segment.

Mixing memory models is also an efficient use of program size. If you are using a small memory model (small or medium), then use the far or huge modifiers for data items or functions that would lie outside of the 64K limits. If you are using a large memory model (compact, large, huge), you can still use the far and huge modifiers for large items, but you can also use the near modifier for items small enough to fit within 64K if you want to increase access speed.

16

17

C

File Input and Output in C

C provides two types of file input and output: standard (or high-level) I/O, and system (or low-level) I/O. The standard I/O functions are precisely defined in the ANSI standard, but the system I/O functions, being machine-specific, are not. Both standard and system I/O can be used to handle physical devices such as disks, terminals, MIDI ports, printers, etc.

C treats disk files and devices (printers, the console, and other peripherals) alike. Because most file I/O functions are device-independent, much of their usage is transparent. There may be certain physical limitations, however, such as reading a character from a printer, or "rewinding" the console.

This leads to a major difference between disk files and many devices: most devices cannot support random access to data. Because C can treat file contents either as text or as binary data, this may limit file handling; some devices (instruments, for example) may not be able to handle text. On the other hand, a device "file" can be opened, closed, and reassigned just like a disk file. Both standard and system-level routines should function on both disk files and devices.

Standard I/O and Streams

When working with I/O in C, you will deal with *streams* of bytes that are manipulated as unformatted, formatted, unbuffered, or buffered data in connection with a pointer to the file. The file structure for these streams is in stdio.h.

Streams should behave the same on all systems (making them portable), but files may not. Standard streams usually are available as stdout (standard output-terminal), stdin (standard input-keyboard), and stderr (standard error output-terminal). Other streams may be stdaux (standard auxiliary device-serial port) or stdprn (standard device-printer).

If input is buffered, the stream information is stored temporarily in an array of bytes called a *buffer*. This increases the speed of retrieving and saving data because these operations are done in blocks instead of byte by byte. Buffering can be set with setbuf(), setvbuf(), or with the system constant BUFSIZE (in stdio.h). Buffering can be done a line at a time or a block at a time. The buffer is emptied (flushed) when it gets full, when the fflush() function is called, when the file is closed, or when the program ends.

If a stream does not already exist, one can be opened or created with fopen(). The pointer returned always should be checked to see if it is NULL, which signifies that a problem occurred.

fopen() opens the file using the mode provided. The default mode is text. Table 17.1 gives the symbols used to designate file modes.

Table 17.1. Symbols for file modes.

Symbol	File mode
r	Read
w	Write
a	Append
rb	Read (binary file)
wb	Write (binary file)
ab	Append (binary file)
r+, w+, a+	Read or write
rb+, wb+, ab+	Open for read/write (binary file)

A file can be opened in either text or binary mode. *Text* mode generally consists of data in the form of lines of characters that may have newlines at the end. *Binary* mode is a sequence of bytes rather than characters and represents data as it is stored in memory.

A file position indicator normally is placed at position 0 (beginning of the file) when a file is opened. The function ftell() reports the current indicator position, and fseek() moves the indicator to a certain position. Using these functions allows for random access of streams instead of the normal sequential access. Another function, rewind(), puts the file indicator back at the beginning of the file.

When a file is opened, data can be read and written in text mode as an unformatted or formatted character or string or as a record using the functions in Table 17.2.

Table 17.2. Stream input/output for standard I/O.

	Character	String	Formatted	Record
Reading	fgetc,	fgets,	fscanf,	fread
	getc	gets	scanf	
Writing	fputc,	fputs,	fprintf,	fwrite
	putc	puts	printf	

The end-of-line (a newline or ASCII decimal 10 character) in a standard C file is represented in DOS as a carriage-return/line-feed pair and consists of ASCII decimal 13 and 10. The end-of-file may also be different between text and binary modes. In text files, it is usually an ASCII decimal 26 (Ctrl-Z). In binary files, it is determined by the file length from system information. The functions feof() and eof() can be used to detect this condition.

Errors can be detected with ferror() and perror(). They can be cleared with clearerr(). When processing is finished, a stream may be closed using fclose().

System I/O for Files

Low-level I/O involves using *file handles* (an integer value representing the file) instead of streams (pointers). The same standard system files are available as handles, as shown in Table 17.3.

Table 17.3. Standard file handles.

File	Handle
stdin	0
stdout	1
stderr	2
stdaux	3
stdprn	4

The data is not formatted or buffered by the system. Buffering can be done by the programmer by using variables, memory manipulation routines, and so on. The file can be opened using open(), which returns a handle if no problems occur. The file can also be subject to various modes of operation set by using flags, as shown in Table 17.4.

Table 17.4. Flags for file modes.

Flag	Significance
O_APPEND	Position file pointer at end of file
O_CREAT	Create a new file
O_RDONLY	Open for reading only
O_RDWR	Use for both reading and writing
O_TRUNC	Open an existing file and truncate it to a length of 0
O_WRONGLY	Open for writing only
O_BINARY	Open in binary mode
O_TEXT	Open in text mode

> **Note:** If the O_CREAT flag is being used, then one of these
> read/write conditions must be added to open():
>
> S_IWRITE   writing permitted
> S_IREAD   reading permitted
> S_IREAD ¦ S_IWRITE   reading and writing permitted

The read() function obtains information from the file, and
write() puts data in the file. The function tell() returns the
position of the file indicator, and lseek() can position the
indicator at a particular location. Error conditions are detected
with perror(). Use the routine close() to close the file properly.

> **Note:** Do *not* mix standard and system file access when
> working with an open file; you might lose data or generate
> unpredictable results.

Console and Port I/O

17

This portion of I/O is specific to MS-DOS. The conio.h header
file contains declarations and prototypes. The routines specific to
console and port I/O are summarized in Table 17.5.

Table 17.5. Summary of console and port I/O.

Function	Result
cgets()	Retrieves string from console
cscanf()	Retrieves data from console
getch()	Retrieves character from console
getche()	Retrieves character from console
ungetc()	Puts character back into keyboard buffer so that it can be reread
cprintf()	Displays data on-screen

Function	Result
cputs()	Displays a string on-screen
putch()	Displays a character on-screen
kbhit()	Checks keyboard buffer for keystrokes
inp()	Inputs to a port
outp()	Reads from a port

The console and port devices do not have to be opened or closed, unlike normal streams and files. They are not compatible with the standard or system level routines, so problems could occur if used in conjunction with them.

18

C Keywords

Table 18.1 lists the keywords defined by the ANSI C standard and used by all C compilers. The table also lists some additional keywords reserved by microcomputer implementations of C compilers but not defined in the ANSI standard.

Table 18.1. C keywords.

ANSI Standard Keywords

auto	double	intstruct	
break	else	long	switch
case	enum	register	typedef
char	extern	return	union
const	float	short	unsigned
continue	for	signed	void
default	goto	sizeof	volatile
do	if	static	while

Additional Keywords for Microcomputers

asm	_ds	fortran	near
_cs	_es	huge	pascal
cdecl	far	interrupt	_ss

C Keywords for Microcomputers

18

asm

Used by some compilers to denote the inclusion of in-line assembly code within routines. asm has the form

```
asm <opcode> <operands> <;
```

or

```
newline>
```

as in

```
asm push ds;
```

You may also need to use a command-line option or statement such as #pragma inline to use asm.

auto

The default storage class (local scope) for most function variables. The variable exists only for the duration of the block in which it is defined.

break

Used to exit unconditionally from a for, while, do ... while loop, or from a case section of a switch statement. Within a switch statement, the break clause in a case section signals the compiler to quit executing any remaining case sections and exit the switch statement. For example:

```
for (count = 1; count < 255; ++count) {
    inchar = getchar();
    if (inchar == ESC)
        break;
    inchar = toupper(inchar);
    printf("%c", inchar);
}
```

If inchar does not equal escape, it is converted to uppercase and displayed if "printable." If it is equal to escape, control goes to the end of the loop, and it is executed again if conditions permit.

case

A section (a specific match) within a switch statement. Because matches cannot be made into ranges, each individual case must be listed in C. See the switch statement.

cdecl

Compilers normally allow you to call routines in other languages. Identifiers are used by the linker in their original form (uppercase, lowercase, or mixed) and are preceded with an underscore. The order in which function parameters are obtained from the stack depends upon the language. C reads from the right to the left; Pascal, from left to right. Using the cdecl modifier in front of an identifier or function states that the normal C conventions should be used instead of those of another language. See also the pascal modifier.

char

A simple variable type representing ASCII characters. char has a length of one byte.

const

A modifier that means the variable's value cannot be changed during program execution.

continue

Causes the compiler to jump immediately to the beginning of the loop to proceed with execution, leaving remaining lines after the continue statement to the end of the loop unexecuted. continue is similar to the break statement.

continue can make programs hard to read. For example,

```
while (color != red) {
    incolor /= 2;
    if (incolor >= DARKGRAY)
    continue;
    scrnwrite(bkgndcolor,
        incolor, "*");
}
```

causes the scrnwrite statement to be skipped if incolor has a value greater than or equal to DARKGRAY; the loop is repeated as long as color does not equal red.

18

default

Used as the last part of a switch statement and is the "normal" case executed when all other cases have not been met. See the `switch` statement.

do

Used in conjunction with the word `while` to form a loop in which conditions are not checked until the end of the loop instead of at the beginning, which is the usual case for a `while` loop. The loop code is executed at least once. If more than one statement is needed between the `do` and `while` clauses, they should be enclosed in braces (`{}`).

double

A data type signifying decimal values of double precision.

else

Part of an `if` clause (see `if`).

enum

A data type allowing formation of lists of objects, each with a particular integer value. Useful for working with a series of items such as error codes, colors, or other resources normally specified by `#define` statements before.

extern

A modifier that tells the compiler the variable or function has been declared elsewhere in the program—usually in a separate module. It usually is not used with function declarations in ANSI-compatible compilers because function prototyping can be used instead.

For example, if the variable `char carname[20]` were declared in a file, then referred to in another file, it would appear as `extern char`

18

carname[] in the second file, and the compiler and linker would know to look outside the present module and find the original declaration and obtain the size.

far

A keyword used by microcomputer installations of C compilers as a modifier for pointers and functions. far means the pointer uses 32 bits instead of 16, allowing reference to data anywhere within the address space on the 80x86/8 processors. See the section "Memory Models and Memory Management."

float

A type modifier for variables of type float.

for

A common statement in C. With a for statement, variables can be initialized and incremented within the body of the for loop. For example:

```
for (count = 1; count <= screenwidth; ++count)
    {
    printf("@");
    get_another_char();
}
```

The general form is

```
for (initialization; condition checking; increment or
decrement);
```

goto

A keyword that causes a jump to a specific program statement having the same label used in the goto. Labels must end with a colon. Unlike older languages, goto in C cannot go outside of the function in which it is used. This keyword makes understanding and maintaining the code more difficult and should be avoided if at all possible.

18

huge

An 80x86/8-specific modifier forcing a pointer variable or function to use 32 bits instead of 16 (consisting of a segment address and offset within the segment). huge uses a *normalized* pointer, which means that as much of its value as possible is placed into the segment address portion of the pointer. Consequently, pointers pointing to the same address can be compared without error. huge also allows manipulation of data larger than 64K in size. See the section "Memory Models and Memory Management."

if

A common C statement of the general form

```
if (condition)
    {
    block1;
    }
else
    {
    block2;
}
```

or

```
if (condition) {
    block1;
}
else {
    block2;
}
```

where the blocks consist of single or multiple statements. Braces are not required if the blocks are single statements. The portion starting with else is also optional. The if statement is executed if the condition evaluates to something other than 0 (false). If an else clause is used, block 1 is executed if the condition is true (value of 1); otherwise, the else section (block 2) is performed. An else belongs to the last if statement unless braces are used to set off the code block. For example:

```
if (first_condition)
    if (second_condition)
```

```
            if (third_condition)
                action1();
        else
            action2();
        else
            action3();
```

The indentation shows that the programmer intends for action2() to be called if second_condition is false. But the compiler pairs the first else statement with the statement

```
if (third_condition)
```

because that if statement is the most recent one not yet paired with an else. Similarly, the second else is paired with the second-most-recent if statement so that action3() is called if second_condition is false.

This code is more clearly expressed using braces as follows:

```
if (condition)
    {
    if (second_condition)
        {
        if (third_condition)
            action1();
        else
            action2();
        }
    else
        action3();
}
```

or

```
if (condition) {
    if (second_condition) {
        if (third_condition)
            action1();
        else
            action2();
    }
    else
        action3();
}
```

18

int

A type identifier for specifying integer variables.

interrupt

A non-ANSI keyword acting as a function modifier signifying a system interrupt routine for use as an interrupt handler. Memory-resident programs, graphics routines, real-time data acquisition, timing functions, and other programs doing special keyboard activity use these types of routines.

long

A data type keyword for extra-precision integers.

near

An 80x86/8-specific, default pointer and function modifier requiring use of 16 bits. Allows access to memory only within a 64K segment. See the section "Memory Models and Memory Management."

pascal

A modifier for functions and identifiers signaling the compiler to use Pascal conventions, such as working with function parameters on the stack from left to right, instead of C conventions. See cdecl.

register

A storage modifier that forces the compiler to try to place the integer or character into its registers instead of into normal memory. This causes increases in speed of execution and efficiency, especially with loop counters and pointers. You cannot use the & operator on register variables.

18

return

Causes the end of a function and results in a value as specified in the function declaration. For example:

```
char getanswer(void);
{
    char achar = 'N';
    while (achar != ESC){
        achar = toupper(getchar());
        if (achar == 'Y' || achar == 'N')
            return(achar);
        else
            return('\0');
    }
}
```

This function returns either the character Y, N, or \0 if the character obtained does not equal Y or N. Any code after the return is not executed.

sizeof

An operator that returns the size of the data object given it as a parameter. sizeof is useful in helping to produce portable code between systems or to determine storage requirements.

signed

A data type modifier in ANSI C for character and integer types; the value may or may not use a plus sign (+) or a minus sign (–).

short

A modifier used with integers; short is usually the same as int on most machines.

static

A storage modifier that tells the compiler to retain the variable or function for the duration of the program. The variable retains its previous value between function calls.

18

struct

Used to create complex variables/types ("records" in other languages) composed of "fields" or "members" of various types. They allow data abstraction and encapsulation of data. See the section "Data Types and Variables" for more information.

switch

A multi-branching statement that more efficiently takes the place of a series of nested if...else statements in C. switch is well-adapted to go through a series of actions, such as for menu selection, keyboard input, filters, and so on. For example:

```
menuselection =
        toupper(getchar());
    switch (menuselection)
    {
    case 'A' :open_file(filename);
        break;
    case 'B' :read_file(filename);
        parse_input();
        display_text();
        close_file(filename);
        break;
    case 'C' :write_to_file(filename);
        close_file(filename);
        break;
    case ESC :
    case 'Q' :quit();
        break;
    default :  warn("Selection not valid\n");
}
```

This switch statement allows four valid inputs to a menu selection, with other characters (default) issuing a warning message.

18

Note: Either an escape (decimal 27) or Q can be entered to leave the menu. Each individual instance of input must be specified; you cannot use a range or list of items separated by commas. Cases must be constants and not variables.

The break statements cause the compiler to drop immediately to the end of the switch statement rather than examine any remaining case sections. The default clause is optional in a switch statement, but you may receive a run-time error if all cases are not provided.

typedef

A keyword that is considered a storage class modifier, but it allows the "creation" (actually the renaming of a preexisting type) of a new variable and function types in C using either simple or complex units. The syntax is

```
typedef <data type> <new name>;
```

For example:

```
typedef int BOOLEAN;
```

Creating a variable using the new type would be

```
BOOLEAN done;
```

which then could take an integer value (0 or 1 is wanted in this case). typedef allows detail-hiding and data abstraction to protect others from information to which they may not be privy and makes code more readable.

union

A complex data type in C where one variable out of all variables listed in the union is used at any particular time. All variables would start at the same memory location (overlay one another) if they could be used at once.

Enough storage is allocated for the largest member regardless of which is used. This allows efficient storage and manipulation of data where its type is not known until run time—for example, a field on a data-entry screen or data from certain files. union is similar to the struct statement in usage.

18

For example,

```
union numtype
      {
      short anint;
      long  along;
      float afloat;
      } xnum;
```

makes a type where an integer, a long, or a float can be stored at a single location (but only one at a time). The data is aligned on appropriate boundaries. It is convenient to use typedef with union definitions, causing the example above to be

```
typedef union numtype
      {
      short anint;
      long along;
      float afloat;
      } NUMBERTYPE;
```

It is up to the programmer to keep track of which data type is being used. One way to do this is to enclose the union within a struct with two fields: a "tag" field (identifying which member is currently used) and the union, as in the following example:

```
struct num {
      char datatype;
      NUMBERTYPE anum;
      } anynum;
```

Now, a switch statement could be written to cover each data type to be used (that is, inputting I for integer and then referring to anynum.anum.anint; or inputting L for long and referring to anynum.anum.along; or inputting F for float and referring to anynum.anum.afloat).

unsigned

A type modifier that signals the compiler to use only positive values and 0 for the data type, such as int, char, and long, but which doubles the effective upper range of the type. See Chapter 13, "Data Types and Variables."

void

A new ANSI C keyword with multiple uses:

◆ It can be used as a function type to signify the function does not return anything:

```
void clearscreen(void);
```

◆ It can be used to denote an empty parameter list to aid the compiler in error checking:

```
int display_text(void);
```

◆ It can be used to make "generic" pointers compatible with any other type. The generic pointers cannot be "dereferenced" with the * operator:

```
void *genericptr;
```

A compiler not yet using void can use the statement #define void; to compensate.

volatile

A data type modifier that tells the compiler the variable can be changed at any time either within the program or even by factors outside the program, such as hardware functions concerning the real-time clock, serial ports, keyboards, and so on.

while

A commonly used loop in languages. For example:

```
while (!eof(filename)) {
    parse_input();
    make_new_file(outfile);
    close_file();
    quit();
}
```

where the actions take place as long as the end-of-file condition is not reached. The loop is executed as long as the condition(s) after the while keyword are true. The loop may never be executed if the conditions are false starting out. The braces are not needed if a single statement is executed.

_cs, _ds, _es, _ss

These are special modifiers within 8088/86 compilers used with pointers to indicate certain segments should be used. Turbo C permits additional "pseudo-variables" to access all registers (_AH, _AL, etc.) directly. These rarely are used unless you are doing hardware-related work such as graphics, interrupt routines, and so on.

19

C Functions

Functions are the building blocks of C programs. Functions allow a simple method of referring to a block of code without repeating each and every line of that block. The general form for a function declaration is

```
<return_type> <function_name>(<parameters>)
{
    statements;
    [return();]
}
```

where <return_type> is the type of value the function returns, such as int, char *, struct *, or void if no value is returned; and <function_name> is the name of the function, such as strcmp or drawdragon. The <parameters> section is enclosed in parentheses and is void if no parameters are specified. A parameter is specified by its type and parameter name (the parameter name may be optional). One or more parameters can be cited for a function: char *fststr, for example. The body of the function consists of one or more statements enclosed in braces. If the <return_type> is not void, then a return statement must yield a value the same type as <return_type>.

main()

In a typical C program, there is a special function called main(), which is the primary function of the program and which calls all other functions. It is usually the first function of a program but does not necessarily need to be. main() normally takes the form

```
void(or int) main (void)
    {
    statements;
    }
```

main() usually has no parameters unless the programmer wants to refer to command-line arguments. In such a case, the form for main() is

```
void (or int) main(int argc, char *argv[])
    {
    statements;
    }
```

Note: The old form (pre-ANSI C) usually was

```
main(argc, argv)
    int argc;
    char *argv[];
    {
    statements;
    }
```

where argc (argument count) is the traditional name for the number of arguments stored as an integer, and argv (argument vector) is an array of character pointers to arguments. (noargs could be used for argc, and argstring could be used for argv.)

Function Prototyping

Another important feature of ANSI C is hinted at in the first form of main()—*function prototyping.* When function prototypes are used, the parameters are specified within the parameter list when the function is first declared instead of being written below the function name. The minimum specification is the type of the parameter

```
void main(int, char *[]);
```

or the actual parameter names can be included:

```
void main(int argc,
    char *argv[]);
```

A function prototype tells the compiler what to look for when it finds the actual definition of the function or a call to the function. Parameters can be checked for proper type and number whenever the function is called, thereby reducing errors. Prototypes also assist the compiler in knowing whether to use near, far, or huge pointers when compiling under different memory models.

Function prototypes are nothing more than the first line of a function definition (minus the body) and typically are placed together near the beginning of the program's source before the function main() or in a header file. The declaration must match

19

the actual definition of the function later in the source although parameter names may differ or be missing entirely. Prototypes for the library functions are found in the header (.h) files included with the compiler. The header files must be #included in your source code.

When prototyping is turned on, if you try to use a function without the appropriate header file, you may get an error message.

C Standard Library Functions

The ANSI C standard provides for the definitions of numerous routines expected to be in the compiler library. This helps to provide added portability when writing for different systems because the functions are expected to take the same parameters, return the same values, and act the same whether you are writing for an IBM PC, a VAX system, etc.

The standard library is divided into 10 main categories: I/O (input/output), string and character, mathematical, time and date, general utilities, character handling, diagnostics, nonlocal jumps, signal handling, and variable argument routines. Many library functions have been taken from the K&R (Kernighan and Ritchie) definition of C. Other functions are from the UNIX operating system, and still others are new to all systems.

Functions related to a category are placed in separate header files. Standard header files as defined by ANSI C are the following:

assert.h	limits.h	signal.h	string.h
ctype.h	locale.h	stdarg.h	time.h
errno.h	math.h	stddef.h	
float.h	setjmp.h	stdio.h	

Functions Covered in This Chapter

The functions covered in the following sections are listed in Table 19.1. A function description consists of the following:

◆ Function prototype (function name, parameters, and return value).

◆ The #include file as defined in the ANSI C standard. This describes what is needed for proper compiler recognition of the function. Compiler differences in the #include file are noted.

◆ A brief description of the function.

◆ Related functions (families of routines similar in syntax or usage).

◆ Any "partner" functions that normally are used with the function to cause it to work more reliably than if used alone.

Table 19.1. C functions covered in this chapter.

Diagnostics (assert.h)

assert()

Character Handling Functions (ctype.h)

isalnum()	isgraph()	isspace()	toupper()
isalpha()	islower()	isupper()	
iscntrl()	isprint()	isxdigit()	
isdigit()	ispunct()	tolower()	

Standard I/O Functions (stdio.h)

clearerr()	fputs()	perror()	setvbuf()
fclose()	fread()	printf()	sprintf()
feof()	freopen()	putc()	sscanf()
ferror()	fscanf()	putchar()	tmpfile()

continues

19

Table 19.1. continued

Standard I/O Functions (stdio.h)

fflush()	fseek()	puts()	tmpnam()
fgetc()	fsetpos()	remove	ungetc()
fgetpos()	fetll()	rename	vfprintf()
fgets()	fwrite()	rewind()	vprintf()
fopen()	getc()	scanf()	vsprintf()
fprint()	getchar()	setbuf()	
fputc()	gets()		

String and Character Handling Functions (string.h)

memchr()	strchrstrlen()	strrchr()	strspn()
memcmp()	strcmp()	strncat()	strstr()
memcpy()	strcoll()	strncmp()	strtok()
memmove()	strcpy()	strncpy()	
memset()	strcspn()	strxfrm()	
strcat()	strerror()	strpbrk()	

Locale-Specific Functions (locale.h)

localeconv()	setlocale()

Mathematical Functions (math.h)

acos()	cosh()	ldexp()	sinh()
asin()	exp()	log()	sqrt()
atan()	fabs()	log10()	tan()
atan2()	floor()	modf()	tanh()
ceil()	fmod()	pow()	
cos()	frexp()	sin()	

Time and Date Functions (time.h)

asctime()	ctime()	gmtime()	mktime()
clock()	difftime()	localtime()	strftime()
			time()

General Utilities (stdlib.h)

abort()	calloc()	malloc()	srand()
abs()	div()	mblen()	strtod()
atexit()	exit()	mbstowcs()	strtol()
atof()	free()	mbtowc()	strtoul()
atoi()	getenv()	qsort()	system()
atol()	labs()	rand()	wcstombs()
bsearch()	ldiv()	realloc()	wctomb()

Nonlocal Jumps (setjmp.h)

longjump()	setjmp()

Signal Handling (signal.h)

raise()	signal()

Variable Function Arguments (stdarg.h)

va_arg()	va_end()	va_start()

Comparison of C Compiler Libraries

Current C compilers often differ from the ANSI standard in their library functions. Most microcomputer implementations of C compilers offer system-specific sets of routines, such as dir.h for directory routines, process.h for creating and terminating new processes, bios.h and dos.h for BIOS, DOS, and other machine-specific routines, alloc.h for memory-handling routines, etc.

In addition, many compilers differ slightly in their arrangement of routine categories, so one routine found in stdlib.h in one compiler may be in alloc.h in another compiler.

19

Note: The value EOF is used when end-of-file is reached during file operations. The value of EOF is normally –1, but it may have other values.

Diagnostics—assert.h

The assert() function tests the conditions represented by expression and prints a message of the format.

Prototype: void assert(int expression);

Include file: assert.h

Related functions: abort()

Returns: None

For example,

Assertion failed: file <filename>, line <linenum>

where file and line number refer to the source file where the call to assert occurred. If assert fails, it will call the function abort to end the program. The normally undefined name NDEBUG can be defined to make any calls to assert ineffective.

Character Handling Functions—ctype.h

A character (char) variable also can be used as a parameter for these functions and is evaluated in the same way as the expected integer parameter.

isalnum()

Checks whether a character is alphanumeric (A-Z, a-z, 0-9).

Prototype: int isalnum(int c);

Include file: ctype.h

19

Related functions: isalpha(), iscntrl(), isdigit(),
isgraph(), islower(), isprint(), ispunct(), isspace(),
isupper(), isxdigit()

Returns: Nonzero value if alphanumeric, otherwise 0

isalpha()

Checks whether a character is a letter of the alphabet (A-Z, a-z).

Prototype: int isalpha(int c);

Include file: ctype.h

Related functions: isalnum(), iscntrl(), isdigit(),
isgraph(), islower(), isprint(), ispunct(), isspace(),
isupper(), isxdigit()

Returns: Nonzero value if in alphabet, otherwise 0

iscntrl()

Checks whether a character is a control character or the delete character (decimal 0 to 31, and 127).

Prototype: int iscntrl(int c);

Include file: ctype.h

Related functions: isalnum(), isalpha(), isdigit(),
isgraph(), islower(), isprint(), ispunct(), isspace(),
isupper(), isxdigit()

Returns: Nonzero value if control character, otherwise 0

isdigit()

Checks whether a character is a digit (0-9).

Prototype: int isdigit(int c);

Include file: ctype.h

Related functions: isalnum(), isalpha(), iscntrl(),
isgraph(), islower(), isprint(), ispunct(), isspace(),
isupper(), isxdigit()

Returns: Nonzero value if a digit, otherwise 0

isgraph()

Checks whether a character is a printable character, excluding the space character (decimal 32).

Prototype: `int isgraph(int c);`

Include file: `ctype.h`

Related functions: `isalnum()`, `isalpha()`, `iscntrl()`, `isdigit()`, `islower()`, `isprin ()`, `ispunct()`, `isspace()`, `isupper()`, `isxdigit()`

Returns: Nonzero value if printable, otherwise 0

islower()

Checks whether a character is a lowercase letter (a-z).

Prototype: `int islower(int c);`

Include file: `ctype.h`

Related functions: `isalnum()`, `isalpha()`, `iscntrl()`, `isdigit()`, `isgraph()`, `isprint()`, `ispunct()`, `isspace()`, `isupper()`, `isxdigit()`

Returns: Nonzero value if lowercase, otherwise 0

va_end	**strtoul**
va_start	**tmpfile**
vfprintf	**tmpnam**
vprintf	
vsprint	

Again, it should be noted that the compilers offer many extra functions not in the ANSI C Draft Standard, especially for DOS compatibility, process control, graphics, etc. In addition, the compilers may include additional functions when the Draft is finalized.

Diagnostics—assert.h

The `assert()` function tests the conditions represented by expression and prints a message of the format.

Prototype: `void assert(int expression);`

Include file: `assert.h`

Related functions: `abort`

Returns: None

For example,

`Assertion failed: file <filename>, line <linenum>`

where `file` and `line number` refer to the source file where the call to `assert` occurred. If `assert` fails, it will call the function `abort` to end the program. The normally undefined name NDEBUG can be defined to make any calls to `assert` ineffective.

Character Handling Functions—ctype.h

A character (`char`) variable also can be used as a parameter for these functions and is evaluated in the same way as the expected integer parameter.

isalnum()

Checks whether a character is alphanumeric (A-Z, a-z, 0-9).

Prototype: `int isalnum(int c);`

Include file: `ctype.h`

Related functions: `isalpha()`, `iscntrl()`, `isdigit()`, `isgraph()`, `islower()`, `isprint()`, `ispunct()`, `isspace()`, `isupper()`, `isxdigit()`

Returns: Nonzero value if alphanumeric, otherwise 0

19

isalpha()

Checks whether a character is a letter of the alphabet (A-Z, a-z).

Prototype: `int isalpha(int c);`

Include file: `ctype.h`

Related functions: `isalnum()`, `iscntrl()`, `isdigit()`, `isgraph()`, `islower()`, `isprint()`, `ispunct()`, `isspace()`, `isupper()`, `isxdigit()`

Returns: Nonzero value if in alphabet, otherwise 0

iscntrl()

Checks whether a character is a control character or the delete character (decimal 0 to 31, and 127).

Prototype: `int iscntrl(int c);`

Include file: `ctype.h`

Related functions: `isalnum()`, `isalpha()`, `isdigit()`, `isgraph()`, `islower()`, `isprint()`, `ispunct()`, `isspace()`, `isupper()`, `isxdigit()`

Returns: Nonzero value if control character, otherwise 0

isdigit()

Checks whether a character is a digit (0-9).

Prototype: `int isdigit(int c);`

Include file: `ctype.h`

Related functions: `isalnum()`, `isalpha()`, `iscntrl()`, `isgraph()`, `islower()`, `isprint()`, `ispunct()`, `isspace()`, `isupper()`, `isxdigit()`

Returns: Nonzero value if a digit, otherwise 0

isgraph()

Checks whether a character is a printable character, excluding the space character (decimal 32).

Prototype: `int isgraph(int c);`

Include file: `ctype.h`

Related functions: `isalnum()`, `isalpha()`, `iscntrl()`, `isdigit()`, `islower()`, `isprint()`, `ispunct()`, `isspace()`, `isupper()`, `isxdigit()`

Returns: Nonzero value if printable, otherwise 0

islower()

Checks whether a character is a lowercase letter (a-z).

Prototype: `int islower(int c);`

Include file: `ctype.h`

Related functions: `isalnum()`, `isalpha()`, `iscntrl()`, `isdigit()`, `isgraph()`, `isprint()`, `ispunct()`, `isspace()`, `isupper()`, `isxdigit()`

Returns: Nonzero value if lowercase, otherwise 0

isprint()

Checks whether a character is printable (decimal 32-126).

Prototype: `int isprint(int c);`

Include file: `ctype.h`

Related functions: `isalnum()`, `isalpha()`, `iscntrl()`, `isdigit()`, `isgraph()`, `islower()`, `ispunct()`, `isspace()`, `isupper()`, `isxdigit()`

Returns: Nonzero value if printable, otherwise 0

19

ispunct()

Checks whether a character is a punctuation character, which in this function means any printable character that is neither a control character nor an alphanumeric character (decimal 32-47, 58-63, 91-96, and 123-126).

Prototype: `int ispunct(int c);`

Include file: `ctype.h`

Related functions: `isalnum()`, `isalpha()`, `iscntrl()`, `isdigit()`, `isgraph()`, `islower()`, `isprint()`, `isspace()`, `isupper()`, `isxdigit()`

Returns: Nonzero value if punctuation, otherwise 0

isspace()

Checks whether a character is whitespace (space, carriage return, horizontal or vertical tab, new line, or form feed).

Prototype: `int isspace(int c);`

Include file: `ctype.h`

Related functions: `isalnum()`, `isalpha()`, `iscntrl()`, `isdigit()`, `isgraph()`, `islower()`, `isprint()`, `ispunct()`, `isupper()`, `isxdigit()`

Returns: Nonzero value is whitespace, otherwise 0

isupper()

Checks whether a character is an uppercase character (A-Z).

Prototype: `int isupper(int c);`

Include file: `ctype.h`

Related functions: `isalnum()`, `isalpha()`, `iscntrl()`, `isdigit()`, `isgraph()`, `islower()`, `isprint()`, `ispunct()`, `isspace()`, `isxdigit()`

Returns: Nonzero value if uppercase, otherwise 0

19

isxdigit()

Checks whether a character is a valid hexadecimal digit (0-9, A-F, a-f).

Prototype: `int isxdigit(int c);`

Include file: `ctype.h`

Related functions: `isalnum(), isalpha(), iscntrl(), isdigit(), isgraph(), islower(), isprint(), ispunct(), isspace(), isupper()`

Returns: Nonzero value if hexidecimal, otherwise 0

tolower()

Converts a character into a lowercase character (a-z) if possible. There is also a macro _tolower.

Prototype: `int tolower(int c);`

Include file: `ctype.h`

Related functions: `toupper(), _tolower(), _toupper()`

Returns: Character converted to lowercase or unchanged character

toupper()

Converts a character into an uppercase character (A-Z) if possible. The macro _toupper is also available.

Prototype: `int toupper(int c);`

Include file: `ctype.h`

Related functions: `tolower(), _toupper(), _tolower()`

Returns: Character converted to uppercase or unchanged character

19

Standard I/O Functions— stdio.h

clearerr()

This function is used to reset error conditions so that the same error is not continuously reported by another function such as ferror. The end-of-file indicator is also set to 1 by clearerr.

Prototype: void clearerr(FILE *stream)

Include file: stdio.h

Related functions: perror(), feof(), rewind()

Partner functions: ferror()

Returns: None

fclose()

Closes the file stream. Normally, all buffers associated with the file are flushed to disk before closing. The buffers are freed to the memory pool unless set by setbuf or setvbuf. It is an error to try to close a file that is already closed.

Prototype: int fclose(FILE *stream);

Include file: stdio.h

Related functions: fflush(), freopen()

Partner functions: fopen()

Returns: Zero (0) if successful or error as integer value

feof()

Checks for end-of-file of the connected stream's file indicator. When end-of-file is reached (by reading past the end of the file), feof continues to return a nonzero value until the file indicator is moved by using fseek(), rewind(), or another similar function or until the stream's error status has been cleared using clearerr().

This is easier to use than checking the value of `getc()` when working with a file. `eof()` performs the same type function but on a file handle. `feof` is especially useful with binary files.

Prototype: `int feof(FILE *stream);`

Include file: `stdio.h`

Related functions: `ferror()`, `eof()`, `getc()`, `putc()`

Partner functions: `fseek()`, `rewind()`, or `clearerr()`

Returns: Zero (0); but when end-of-file is reached, returns a nonzero value

ferror()

This function tests the stream to see whether a read or write error has occurred. `ferror` remains set until `clearerr()` or `rewind()` is called to reset it, or until the file is closed as with `fclose()`.

Prototype: `int ferror(FILE *stream);`

Include file: `stdio.h`

Related functions: `eof()`, `getc()`, `putc()`, `perror()`

Partner functions: `clearerr()`, `rewind()`, or `fclose()`

Returns: Zero (0); but when error has occurred, returns a nonzero value

fflush()

Writes the contents of the stream's output buffer to a file and clears the buffer's contents. The stream remains open. It is not widely used, because terminating a program or closing a file typically flushes the buffers. A recent change to the ANSI draft standard states that using `fflush(NULL)` would be the same as flushing all buffers of any files open.

Prototype: `int fflush(FILE *stream);`

Include file: `stdio.h`

19

Related functions: `fopen()`, `freopen()`, `fclose()`, `fread()`, `fwrite()`

Returns: Zero (0); but when write error occurs, returns a nonzero value

fgetc()

This function reads the next character from the stream. Use `feof` to determine if end-of-file has been reached when that conditions occurs.

Prototype: `int fgetc(FILE *stream);`

Include file: `stdio.h`

Related functions: `getc()`, `getchar()`, `fread()`

Partner functions: `feof()`

Returns: Character as integer value, or `EOF` if end-of-file is reached

fgets()

`fgets` reads characters from the stream until it has gotten n-1 characters, then stores them in the string pointed to by `*s`. `fgets` continues until it detects a newline, reaches EOF, or reaches the n-1 limit.

If a newline is detected, it is kept as part of the string. If a null pointer is returned, use `feof()` or `ferror()` to tell what the error is. `fgets` is safer to use than `gets` because a limit can be set on the length of input.

Prototype: `char *fgets(char *s, int n, FILE *stream);`

Include file: `stdio.h`

Related functions: `gets()`

Partner functions: `feof()`, `ferror()`

Returns: String `*s` unless an error occurs, then returns a null pointer

fgetpos()

The function fgetpos is new in ANSI C and stores the position of the file indicator from stream in *pos. fsetpos then can be used to set the file indicator position. fgetpos was designed to work with files larger than what could be handled by fseek and ftell. errno is a variable or macro (lvalue) that may be checked for an error code returned by ferror, fgetpos, or a similar function. To be used correctly, errno should be set to zero before the function call and checked for a new error code after the call.

Prototype: `int fgetpos(FILE *stream, fpos_t *pos);`

Include file: `stdio.h`

Related functions: `fseek()`, `ftell()`

Partner functions: `fsetpos()`

Returns: Positions (*pos) or nonzero value if not successful

fopen()

The function fopen opens the file filename using the mode provided and associates the file with a stream.

Prototype:
`FILE *fopen(const char *filename, constchar *mode);`

Include file: `stdio.h`

Related functions: `freopen()`, `fflush()`

Partner functions: `fclose()`

Returns: Pointer to stream, or null pointer if unsuccessful

The modes for this function are shown in Table 19.2.

19

Table 19.2. Modes for the `fopen` function.

Mode	Definition
r	Read
w	Write
a	Append
rb	Read (binary file)
wb	Write (binary file)
ab	Append (binary file)
r+, w+, a+	Read or write
rb+, wb+, ab+	Open for read/write (binary file))

If no `filename` as given exists, a new file is created; otherwise, the file's contents are erased unless the *a* (append) mode is used.

fprint()

See the special section on the `printf` family later in this section.

Prototype:
```
int fprintf(FILE *stream, const char*format, ...);
```

Include file: `stdio.h`

Related functions: `printf()`, `sprintf()`, `vprintf()`, `putc()`, `puts()`

Returns: Number of characters written, or a negative value (`EOF`) when an error occurs

fputc()

The function `fputc` writes a character to a file pointed to by `stream`. `fputc` basically operates just like `putc`. `putchar` writes the character to the device `stdout`.

Prototype: `int fputc(int c, FILE *stream);`

Include file: `stdio.h`

19

Related functions: `putc()`, `putchar()`, `puts()`, `fputs()`, `fgets()`

Returns: Character just written as an integer, or EOF when an error occurs

fputs()

This function writes to a file an entire string pointed to by `*s`. The similar function, `puts`, writes the string to `stdout`.

Prototype: `int fputs(const char *s, FILE *stream);`

Include file: `stdio.h`

Related functions: `puts()`, `putc()`, `gets()`, `fgets()`

Returns: Nonzero value or EOF when an error occurs

fread()

`fread` reads from a file `nmemb` elements, each of which are of size `size`, and stores them in the buffer pointed to by `*ptr`. `size_t` is an unsigned integer defined in the header file `stddef.h`.

Prototype:
`size_t fread(void *ptr, size_t size, size_t nmemb, FILE *stream);`

Include file: `stdio.h`

Related functions: `fwrite()`, `fscanf()`, `getc()`, `gets()`

Returns: Number of elements successfully read or 0 when an error occurs

For example,

```
fread((char *)&inputbuf, sizeof(struct bookreference),
100, inputfile);
```

which reads up to 100 "records" (structs) from `inputfile` and stores them in `inputbuf`. After reading, the file indicator is moved to the end of that area.

freopen()

The function freopen replaces stream with filename using mode (r, w, a, rb+, etc.). The stream is closed whether or not it was open. freopen is useful in making changes to the standard devices of stdin, stdout, and stderr.

Prototype: FILE *freopen(const char *filename,
                         const char *mode,
                         FILE *stream);

Include file: stdio.h

Related functions: fopen(), fflush()

Partner functions: fclose()

Returns: Pointer to stream if successful or a null pointer when an error occurs

fscanf()

This function allows formatted input from the file via input fields and converts the input to the specified format. See the special section on the scanf family in this section for more information.

Prototype:
int fscanf(FILE *stream, const char*format, ...);

Include file: stdio.h

Related functions: scanf(), sscanf(), vscanf()

Returns: Number of characters input (including 0), or EOF on error

fseek()

The function fseek positions the file indicator of stream by telling it a starting point (whence) within the file and the distance in bytes (offset) to go from that point, thus allowing random access. The function ftell can be used to calculate offset. ANSI specifies whence as three constants:

19

SEEK_SET = 0 = beginning of the file;
SEEK_CUR = 1 = current position; and
SEEK_END = 2 = end of the file.

In order to work with files larger than 64K, offset is (or should be cast to) a long integer. fseek may have problems calculating the correct position within text files unless offset is set to 0L or ftell is used along with SEEK_SET. fseek, therefore, usually is used on binary files. It also clears any prior calls to ungetc or end-of-file.

Prototype:
```
int fseek(FILE *stream, long int offset, int whence);
```

Include file: stdio.h

Related functions: fgetpos(), fsetpos()

Partner functions: ftell()

Returns: Zero (0), or nonzero value if unsuccessful

fsetpos()

This function positions the file indicator of stream at the position pointed to by *pos, which has been calculated by fgetpos. fsetpos was added by the ANSI standard to deal with files too large to handle with fseek and ftell.

Prototype: int fsetpos(FILE *stream, const fpos_t *pos);

Include file: stdio.h

Related functions: fseek(), ftell()

Partner functions: fgetpos(), errno()

Returns: Zero (0), or a nonzero value upon error

ftell()

The function ftell reports the current position of the file indicator of stream—from the beginning of the file in most cases. If an error occurs, errno should be used to check what actually happened.

19

Prototype: `long int ftell(FILE *stream);`

Include file: `stdio.h`

Related functions: `fgetpos(), fsetpos()`

Partner functions: `fseek(), errno()`

Returns: Position from the beginning of file as a long int; −1 on error

fwrite()

This function writes nmemb, each with a size of `size` to the `stream` beginning at the position pointed to by *ptr.

Prototype: `size_t fwrite(const void *ptr, size_t size, size_t nmemb, FILE *stream);`

Include file: `stdio.h`

Related functions: `fopen(), getc(), gets(), putc(), puts()`

Partner functions: `fread()`

Returns: Number of items actually written, or a short count upon error (< `nmemb`)

For example:

```
fwrite((char *)&inputbuf, sizeof(struct bookreference),
100, inputfile);
```

After writing to the file, the file indicator is moved to the end of that area.

getc()

getc reads a character from `stream` and readies the file indicator for the next character. Use feof to test the end-of-file condition. getc is a macro and is otherwise the same as fgetc. ungetc can push a character back onto the file to be read again by getc.

Prototype: `int getc(FILE *stream);`

Include file: `stdio.h`

Related functions: `putc()`, `fgetc()`, `fgetchar()`, `getchar()`, `gets()`, `puts()`, `fgets()`, `ungetc()`

Partner functions: `feof()`, `(ungetc)`

Returns: Integer value of character read, or EOF if end-of-file is reached

getchar()

The function `getchar` gets the next character from `stdin` and sets the file indicator to read the next character. You also can use `feof` to check for EOF and `ungetc` to put a character back.

Prototype: `int getchar(void);`

Include file: `stdio.h`

Related functions: `fgetc()`, `getc()`, `putc()`, `fgetchar()`, `gets()`, `puts()`, `fgets()`, `ungetc()`

Partner functions: `feof()`, `(ungetc)`

Returns: Integer value of next character, or EOF

gets()

The function `gets` gets a null-terminated (normal C) string from the device `stdin` and continues reading characters until a newline is reached or until EOF is reached (checked by `feof`). In the case of a newline, the newline is not added to the end of the string. `gets` does have a fault: it is up to the programmer to make sure the buffer (`*s`) is not overflowed because `gets` does no length-checking. `fgets` is safer, therefore, because it reads only $n-1$ characters.

Prototype: `char *gets(char *s);`

Include file: `stdio.h`

Related functions: `getc()`, `fgetc()`, `putc()`, `fgetc()`, `fgetchar()`, `fgets()`, `puts()`, `ungetc()`

19

Partner functions: feof()

Returns: Pointer to string just read, or null pointer if an error occurs

perror()

The function perror prints the string *s on stderr (standard error output device) along with a colon and a space followed by a brief message corresponding to errno, and then a newline.

Prototype: void perror(const char *s);

Include file: stdio.h

Related functions: strerror(), ferror()

Partner functions: errno (actually an integer value)

Returns: None

printf()

See the special section on the printf family later in this section.

Prototype: int printf(const char *format, ...);

Include file: stdio.h

Related functions: fprintf(), sprintf(), vprintf()

Returns: Number of characters output, or 0 if an error occurs

putc()

The function putc writes a character to stream. Error conditions should be checked with feof to see whether that condition actually exists. It is implemented as a macro and functions like fputc.

Prototype: int putc(int c, FILE *stream);

Include file: stdio.h

Related functions: fgetc(), getc(), fgetchar(), gets(), puts(), fgets(), ungetc(), putchar()

Partner functions: feof()

Returns: Character as integer value, or EOF if an error occurs

putchar()

The function putchar writes a character to the device stdout. Error conditions are checked with feof. putchar is also implemented as a macro.

Prototype: int putchar(int c);

Include file: stdio.h

Related functions: fgetc(), getc(), fgetchar(), gets(), puts(), fgets(), ungetc()

Partner functions: feof()

Returns: Character as integer value, or EOF if an error occurs

puts()

The function puts writes a string to the stdout device and adds a newline to the end of the device, even if a newline already exists.

Prototype: int puts(const char *s);

Include file: stdio.h

Related functions: fgetc(), getc(), fgetchar(), gets(), fgets(), ungetc(), putchar(), printf()

Returns: Zero (0), or nonzero (EOF, non-ANSI) value if an error occurs

remove()

This function deletes, erases, or removes the file filename from the system. When filename is open the actions performed are compiler-specific. When filename is removed the file is no longer accessible.

Prototype: int remove(const char *filename);

Include file: stdio.h

19

Related functions: `rename()`

Returns: Zero (0), or nonzero value when an error occurs

rename()

Changes the name of file called `old` to `new`. On the PC, the compiler may allow a different directory in `new` from that in `old` and thereby move the file from one directory to another (the drive, if given, must be the same). If the file name given by `new` already exists, or is open, the actions are compiler-specific.

Prototype: `int rename(const char *old, const char *new);`

Include file: `stdio.h`

Related functions: `remove()`

Returns: Zero (0), or nonzero value if not successful

rewind()

`rewind` moves the file indicator to the beginning of the file `stream` and clears any existing error conditions. It is the same as saying:

`fseek(stream, 0L, SEEK_SET);`

Prototype: `void rewind(FILE *stream);`

Include file: `stdio.h`

Related functions: `fseek()`, `fsetpos()`

Returns: None

scanf()

See the special section on the `scanf` family later in this section.

Prototype: `int scanf(const char *format, ...);`

Include file: `stdio.h`

Related functions: `fscanf()`, `sscanf()`, `vscanf()`

Returns: Number of characters input (including 0) or `EOF` on error

19

setbuf()

The function setbuf allows the programmer to specify a buffer for stream other than the system buffer for file I/O, which is pointed to by *buf and must be BUFSIZE (defined in stdio.h also) in size. The buffer may be NULL, in which case buffering is effectively turned off. Buffering means the characters read and written from a file are stored in a special area (with *buf as the beginning of the area) and worked with as a unit rather than individually; the buffering area is flushed when full. The variable buf should be static or global in scope unless you close the file within the block in which buf is declared.

Prototype: void setbuf(FILE *stream, char *buf);

Include file: stdio.h

Related functions: setvbuf(), fclose()

Partner functions: fopen()

Returns: None

setvbuf()

The function setvbuf establishes a buffer for stream pointed to by *buf with a size that should be BUFSIZE as defined in stdio.h. No buffering occurs if buf is NULL. The third parameter, mode, corresponds to one of three integer constants:

1. _IOFBF = fully buffered

2. _IOLBF = line buffered, or the buffer is flushed after every line, or the buffer is flushed when a newline is detected

3. _IONBF = no buffering.

Prototype: int setvbuf(FILE *stream, char *buf, intmode, size_t size);

Include file: stdio.h

Related functions: setbuf(), fclose()

Partner functions: fopen()

19

Returns: Zero (0) if successful or nonzero value if problems occur

sprintf()

See the special section on the scanf family later in this section.

Prototype: `int sprintf(char *s, const char *format, ...);`

Include file: `stdio.h`

Related functions: `fprintf(), vprintf()`

Returns: Number of characters output, or 0 if an error occurs

sscanf()

See the special section on the scanf family later in this section.

Prototype:
`int sscanf(const char *s, const char *format, ...);`

Include file: `stdio.h`

Related functions: `scanf(), fscanf(), vscanf()`

Returns: Number of characters input (including 0), or EOF on error

tmpfile()

The function tmpfile creates and opens a temporary file in the wb+ mode (binary file with read and write privileges) which will be closed and removed when the program ends. (wb+ is the ANSI standard; other implementations use w+.)

Prototype: `FILE *tmpfile(void);`

Include file: `stdio.h`

Related functions: `tmpnam()`

Partner functions: `fopen()`

Returns: Pointer to stream just created, or null pointer on error

tmpnam()

tmpnam creates a unique file name up to TMP_MAX (in stdio.h) times, which must be at least 25 times. The names will not conflict with any other names and are meant to be temporary. tmpnam creates storage for the name even if *s is NULL.

Prototype: char *tmpnam(char *s);

Include file: stdio.h

Related functions: tmpfile()

Returns: Character pointer to new name *s, or null pointer on failure

ungetc()

This function puts a character (except EOF) back onto stream to be read again by either fgetc, getc, or getchar if file buffering is on, and at least one character already has been read. This is useful for checking to see what is ahead and being able to put it back if needed. Calls to fopen or freopen void any characters in storage to be put back. This also means the file indicator is moved back one position for each character, so functions changing the indicator's position (for example, fseek, fsetpos) affect ungetc's memory also.

Prototype: int ungetc(int c, FILE *stream);

Include file: stdio.h

Related functions: fgetchar(), gets(), puts(), fgets(), putchar()

Partner functions: fgetc(), getc(), or getchar(); fseek(), fopen(), or freopen()

Returns: Integer value of the character, or EOF on error

vfprintf()

See the special section on the printf family later in this section.

19

Prototype: `int vfprintf(FILE *stream,`
`const char *format, va_list arg);`

Include file: `stdio.h`

Related functions: `fprintf()`, `printf()`, `vprintf()`, `vsprintf()`

Returns: Number of characters output, or 0 if error

vprintf()

See the special section on the `printf` family later in this section.

Prototype: `int vprintf(const char *format, va_list arg);`

Include file: `stdio.h`

Related functions: `fprintf()`, `printf()`, `vfprintf()`, `vsprintf()`

Returns: Number of characters output, or 0 if error

vsprintf()

See the special section on the `printf` family later in this section.

Prototype:
`int vsprintf(char *s, const char*format, va_list arg);`

Include file: `stdio.h`

Related functions: `fprintf()`, `printf()`, `vfprintf()`, `vprintf()`

Returns: Number of characters output, or 0 if error

The *printf()* Family

Prototypes:
`int fprintf(FILE *stream, const char *format, ...);`
outputs to a file

`int printf(const  char *format, ...);`
outputs to stdout

`int sprintf(char *s, const char *format,...);`
outputs to a string

```
int vfprintf(FILE *stream, const char *format,
             va_list arg);
```
just like fprintf but accepts variable arguments from va_arg

```
int vprintf(const char *format, va_list arg);
```
just like printf but accepts variable arguments from va_arg

```
int vsprintf(char *s, const char *format,
             va_list arg);
```
just like sprintf but accepts variable arguments from va_arg

Include file: stdio.h

Returns: Although rarely used, the functions do return integer values. Most return the number of characters actually output, or a negative value if an error occurs. For those functions sending output to a string, the terminating null character is not counted in the number of characters output.

Description

This group of functions accepts input formatted according to certain specifications and sends it to different places: files, standard system devices, strings, etc. Some compilers also have other printf functions, such as cprintf, that are not part of the ANSI Draft Standard and send output only to the console (screen).

In this section, each format specification is given, along with other text and applicable escape sequences (for example, \n or \t) as a string. The string does not need to contain any format specifiers if only text is desired. Each variable is then listed in the parameter list when the function is called. These functions are used to a great extent because they deal with output.

fprintf should have a valid stream (file) as the first parameter in order to direct output to the stream; this can include also the standard system devices of stdout and stderr. sprintf causes formatted output to be placed in a string given as the first parameter, so new strings can be created by combining various combinations of other strings. The programmer must also ensure that the size of the string to hold the new output is large enough, or results may be unpredictable.

19

Formatting Standards

The general form of the format specification string is:

```
"% [flags] [width] [.precision]
     [F or N or h or l] type"
```

For example:

```
"%+10.5ld"
```

or

```
"The value is %+10.5ld\n"
```

Type Characters

Table 19.3 shows the format specifications that tell the compiler which type is expected from the argument list. If the argument does not match the format type, the output may not be correct.

Table 19.3. Type characters.

Format Specifier	Constant Example	Explanation
Integers		
d, i	-8324	Signed decimal integers and longs
o	\145	Signed octal integer
u	391	Unsigned decimal integers and longs
x, X	\x65	Unsigned hexidecimal conversion
Floats		
f	81.8174	Signed (double) floating point value
e, E	2.479e3	Signed (double) floating point value with exponential notation
g, G	75.312	Signed (double) float of either e or f format

19

Characters

c	b	Single character
s	"cat"	String
%	%	(actually %%) prints percent sign

Pointers

n	int *nchr	Holds the number of characters output so far
p	anyptr	Prints pointer address: near pointers as OOOO (offset only); far pointers as SSSS:OOOO (segment:offset)

Flag Characters

These characters signify certain output characteristics (see Table 19.4). Right-justification is the default.

Table 19.4. Flag characters.

Format Specifier	Input Example	Explanation
-	%-2.2d	Causes left-justification, padding on the right with blanks
0	%02.4d	Zeros are used to pad instead of spaces if a field length is given
+	%+3.1d	Output always begins with a + or − sign
blank	% 4d	Positive values begin with a blank
#	%#	An alternate number form is used in the conversion of e, E, f, g, G, o, x, and X formats.

Width Specifications

Table 19.5 shows the characters denoting the width of the field in which output is printed. If, for example, eight characters or positions are desired, the format specification would be %8d, and 35.781 would be 35.781. %5s with This is a test. as input would print: This.

Table 19.5. Field width specifications.

Format Specifier	Input Example	Explanation
n	%10s	A minimum of n characters are printed and may be padded to fill any remaining positions. Note strings are not necessarily affected by the width specification; rather, it is the *precision* portion which can cause a different length string to be output. For example, %.4s would cause reference to be output as refe, but %4s would allow the entire string to be output as reference.
*	%*f	The width specifier is supplied by the argument list instead of the format string.

The specifier must appear *before* the argument to be formatted. This would allow the width and precision to be supplied at runtime instead of prior to compilation. For example, %*.*f would require arguments of 5, 3, and 82.1493 and would effectively use a format of %5.3f to cause 82.149 as output.

Precision Specifications

Table 19.6 shows the characters used for precision specifications.

Table 19.6. Precision specifications.

Format Specifier	Explanation
None cited or .0	Default precision is used: d, i, o, u, x, X = 1; e, E, f = 6, nodecimal with .0; g, G = all digits; s = all characters; c = nothing;
.n	n positions are used as output, so the value may or may not be shortened or lengthened
*	The precision is given in the argument list (see Table 19.4)

Input Size Specification

Table 19.7 shows the characters used for specifying the size of input arguments.

Table 19.7. Input size specification.

Format Specifier	Input Example	Explanation
F	%3.3Ff	The argument is considered to be a far pointer (not ANSI C)
N	%3.3Nf	The argument is considered to be a near pointer (not ANSI C)
h	%hd	The argument must be of type short int
l	%ld	The argument must be of type long int
L (ANSI C)	%Le	The argument is of type long double and can be used with e, E, f, g, or G; this may not exist in present compilers

19

Examples

Example 1:

```c
#include <stdio.h>

void main(void)
    {
    int anint = -358;
    float afloat = 877.149;
    char *astring;
    char achar = 'w';
    char bigstring[80];

    /* allocate string pointer, size + 1 for null char */
    astring = (char *)malloc(10);
    astring = "reference";

    printf("The results are:\n");
    printf("Integer = %-d\n", anint);
    /* pads left with 0's instead of spaces  */
    printf("Integer = %06\n", anint);
    printf("Float   = %5.5f\n", afloat);
    printf("Float   = %*.*f\n", 5, 3, afloat);
    printf("String  = %.3s\n", astring);
    /* writes 3 chars of a string in a total field length of
       15 positions with an asterisk afterwards  */
    printf("String  = %15.3s*\n", astring);
    printf("Char    = %c\n", achar);
    printf("Altogether: %-d %5.5 %s %c\n", anint, afloat,
    astring, achar);
    /* this puts output to the stderr device, which may be a
       file  */
    fprintf(stderr, "The example is almost finished.\n");
    sprintf(bigstring, "%s %.4s.", "This is a",
    "testability");
    printf("String  = %s\n", bigstring);
    }
```

causes the following output:

```
The results are:
    Integer = -358
    Integer = -000358
    Float   = 877.14899
    Float   = 877.149
```

```
String  = ref
String  = ref*
Char    = w
Altogether:   -358 877.14899 reference w
String  = This is a test.
```

If you would examine stderr, you would find the following message:

```
The example is almost finished.
```

Example 2:

This example shows the functions vprintf, vfprintf, and vsprintf. These functions allow a variable number of arguments to be used in a call to a user-written function. Your routine then can use the same format strings (that is, "%4.2f") and perform almost the same as printf. vfprintf writes to a file, and vsprintf outputs to a string.

Notice that if you used printf in the routine, you would have to determine beforehand the exact parameters needed by citing the proper format string and matching parameters. With the vprintf functions, however, you do not need to know the exact number. For example, if you want to write a special debug function to print out information during the program to two different files when you don't know just how many parameters you want to use, you could do the following:

```c
#include <stdio.h>
#include <stdargs.h>  /*  <varargs.h> in some compilers */

FILE *outfile; /*  a global file already prepared
foraccepting output, along with stderr
*/

/*  set up your own function similar to printf */
void debug(char *formatstr, ...)
    {
    /* define the arguments type */
    va_list arguments;
```

```
/*  signal start of arguments and last fixed arg */
va_start(arguments, formatstr);
/*  write same information to stderr and outfile */
vfprintf(stderr, formatstr, arguments);
vfprintf(outfile, formatstr, arguments);
/*  clean up with va_end */
va_end(arguments);
}
```

With sample calls such as

```
debug("The problem occurs with the integer type of value
    %d\n" firstinteger);
    /*  example checks loop control and error check */
    if (count1 != 34 && errorcount != 1)
debug("%s and %s are not incrementing.\n",
"count1","errorcount");
```

the output from both debug calls would be sent to both the stderr and the outfile established in the program.

The *scanf()* Family

Prototypes: `int fscanf(FILE *stream,`
                       `const char *format, ...);`

allows input from a file according to the given format,

`int scanf(const char *format, ...);`

allows formatted input from the stdin device, and

`int sscanf(const char *s, const`
          `char *format, ...);`

allows input from the string s, which is formatted.

Many implementations have related functions, such as vscanf, vfscanf, vsscanf, and cscanf, which are not defined in the ANSI Draft Standard.

Include file: `#include <stdio.h>`

Returns: The number of fields successfully processed are returned by these functions, and a negative value (-1 = EOF) is returned if the end-of-file is discovered during input.

Description

This family of functions allows input of values from the keyboard, from a string, or from a file. The format specifications are similar to those used by printf, so only the differences are pointed out here. The function stops reading input when one of the following conditions is met:

1. The next character is EOF.

2. The end of the format string has been reached.

3. A mismatch has occurred between the format string and the input fields or between the control character set and the character input.

Problems with *scanf()*

The functions are prone to error because of mismatches between the format control string and input, an incorrect number of variables to hold the input specified in the format string, or reaching end-of-file. Another common error is omitting the & operator when passing nonpointer arguments to the function during a call. (scanf expects its arguments to be pointers, which are addresses, not values.)

Whitespace in the control string to be matched with whitespace in the input can be a problem also. This means that scanf could even accept input from more than one line, because newlines are considered whitespace. Unfortunately, some compilers leave the newline in the input buffer, and the newline is "hidden" there until the next input, acting like an extra keystroke and throwing things out of whack. You must be careful, therefore, in employing the scanf functions and thoroughly test their usage. Also, you could consider writing your own input functions.

Format Specification

The general form of the format specification string is

```
"% [*] [width] [F or N] [h or l] type"
```

For example:

```
"%4s"
```

All lowercase type characters as from scanf are allowed in ANSI C (%d, %i, %o, %u, %x, %c, %s, %e, %f, %g, and %%).

Note: If %s is used, the string to hold input must be large enough for all characters *and* a terminating null character, which is automatically appended.

Brackets ([ ]) may also be included and are placed in one argument, which is of type char *. The brackets contain a set of characters allowed during input. This makes the brackets useful for field checks, such as allowing only the digits 0-9 ([0123456789]) when inputting unsigned integers.

If the circumflex (^), also called the *top hat* or *caret*, is immediately after the opening bracket, it signals to the compiler to allow negation of input. Any other position in the set has no special meaning.

The right and left brackets may be included if they are immediately at the beginning of the set. This facility is useful for fields not containing whitespace.

The asterisk (*) can function here in assignment suppression. The input field is scanned but not used to fill the next argument in the function parameter list.

Field width may be specified by using an integer value between the % sign and the type—for example, %9f. No precision can be specified.

The same modifiers are allowed as for printf: F, N, h, l, or L.

scanf functions normally stop reading input to a particular field if the width is exceeded, the character does not match what is in the control set, a whitespace character is detected, or there is a format string conflict.

For example:

```
int result;
result = scanf("%3d %5f %10s %1c\n", &anint, &afloat,
               astring, &achar);
```

In the example, if the input is

```
123456 948571 encounter q
```

then anint would equal 123, afloat would equal 456, astring would equal 948571, and achar would equal e.

If the input is

```
123 987.6 correspond zv
```

anint would equal 123, afloat would equal 987.6, astring would equal correspond, and achar would equal z. v would be left over for the next input to a different variable.

Example using *scanf()*

```
#include <stdio.h>

void main(void)
    {
    int anint;
    float afloat;
    char *astring;
    char achar;
    char bigstring[80];
    char newline;
    int result;

    astring = (char *)malloc(10);

    printf("Input an integer:  ");
    result = scanf("%3d\n", &anint);
    newline = getchar();
    printf("The answer is %d  %d\n", result, anint);
    printf("Input a float:  ");
    result = scanf("%5f\n", &afloat);
    newline = getchar();
    printf("The answer is %d  %f\n", result, afloat);
    printf("Input a string:  ");
    result = scanf("%10s\n", astring);
```

19

```
printf("The answer is %d  %s\n", result, astring);
printf("Input a character:  ");
result = scanf("%1c\n", &achar);
printf("The answer is %d  %c\n", result, achar);
printf("Input an integer, float, string, and char:  ");
result = scanf("%3d %5f %10s %1c\n", &anint, &afloat,
               astring, &achar);
printf("They are %d    %d, %f, %s, %c\n", result,
       anint, afloat, astring, achar);
}
```

This example prompts the user for various values according to the parameters of the scanf statements. The results are formatted by scanf and then printed.

String and Character Functions—string.h

memchr()

The function memchr scans the object pointed to by *s for the character c within the first n characters of the object.

Prototype: void *memchr(const void *s, int c, size_t n);

Include file: string.h, or mem.h (non-ANSI)

Related functions: strchr(), strstr()

Returns: Pointer to the located character, or a null pointer if it is not in the object pointed to by s

memcmp()

memcmp compares two strings, s1 and s2, for n number of characters to see whether they differ.

Prototype: int memcmp(const unsigned char *s1, const
                             unsigned char *s2, size_t n);

Include file: string.h, or mem.h (non-ANSI)

Related functions: `strcmp`

Returns: 0 if s1=s2
integer > 0 if s1 > s2
integer < 0 if s1 < s2

memcpy()

The function `memcpy` copies n characters from the memory location pointed to by s2 and puts the characters into the location pointed to by s1. You may run into problems if the two objects overlap; results are undefined in that instance. It is safer to use `memmove` because it works with overlapping objects. Many non-ANSI implementations (called `memccpy`) either return a character pointer instead of a void pointer or take a fourth parameter (positioned third in the argument list), `int val`, which will cause copying to stop if a character of `val` is reached.

Prototype: `void *memcpy(void *s1, const void *s2, size_t n);`

Include file: `string.h`, or `mem.h` (non_ANSI)

Related functions: `memmove()`, `strcpy()`, `strncpy()`

Returns: Void (generic) pointer pointing to s1

memmove()

`memmove` works much the same as `memcpy` by moving n characters from the region pointed to by s2 and putting the characters into the region pointed to by s1. `memmove` works correctly even if s1 and s2 overlap. The effect is as though s2 would be copied into a temporary region first and then copied to the new region.

Prototype: `void *memmove(void *s1, const void *s2, sizt_t n);`

Include file: `string.h`, or `mem.h` (non-ANSI)

Related functions: `memcpy()`, `strcpy()`, `strncpy()`

Returns: Void pointer pointing to s1

19

memset()

The function memset makes (initializes) each character from the beginning of s up to n number of characters the value of c. Its purpose is therefore to initialize memory to a particular value, similar to calloc, which initializes memory to 0 when creating storage for a pointer. You could create a string of 50 dashes:

```
char lineOfDashes[80];
char *result;
result = memset(lineOfDashes, '-', 50);
```

Prototype: void *memset(void *s, int c, size_t n);

Include file: string.h, or mem.h (non-ANSI)

Related functions: calloc(), strcpy(), strncpy(), memcpy()

Returns: Pointer to the object s

strcat()

This function adds the string s2 to the end of string s1, overwriting anything in memory after s1. strcat should, therefore, be large enough to hold both strings, or you may write on top of other valuable data. The null terminator of s1 is replaced by the first character of s2 in the process.

Prototype: char *strcat(char *s1, const char *s2);

Include file: string.h

Related functions: strncat(), strchr(), strcpy(), strncpy()

Returns: Pointer to string s1

strchr()

This function searches the string pointed to by s looking for character c.

Prototype: char *strchr(const char *s, int c);

Include file: string.h

Related functions: memchr(), strstr(), strrstr()

19

Returns: Character pointer to c within the string s, or a null pointer if not found

strcmp()

This function is similar to memcmp and compares s1 to the string s2 to see whether they differ. In total, n number of characters are compared.

Prototype:
```
int strcmp(const unsigned char *s1,
           const unsigned char *s2);
```

Include file: string.h

Related functions: memcmp()

Returns: 0 if s1=s2
integer > 0 if s1 > s2
integer < 0 if s1 < s2

strcoll()

The function strcoll compares two strings according to the locale of the program. In other words, special characters of a foreign language used by the compiler, such as those with accents, diacritical marks, umlauts, and so on, are also taken into consideration. A possible application would be sorting sequences or applications for foreign languages.

Prototype: `int strcoll(const char *s1, const char *s2);`

Include file: string.h

Related functions: strcmp(), strncmp()

Partner functions: strxfrm()

Returns: 0 if s1=s2
integer > 0 if s1 > s2
integer < 0 if s1 < s2

19

strcpy()

This function copies the contents of a string, s2, into the contents of the string given as the first parameter, s1. If the two strings overlap, the results are unpredictable. The copying takes place even if they are of different lengths, and the terminating null character is included. It is used in place of string assignment in other languages, such as Pascal. For example,

```
strcpy(newstring, oldstring);
```

is the same as the following in Pascal:

```
Newstring := Oldstring;
```

Prototype: `char *strcpy(char *s1, const char *s2);`

Include file: `string.h`

Related functions: `strncpy(), memcpy(), memmove()`

Returns: Character pointer to s1

strcspn()

strcspn calculates the number of characters which start from the beginning of the string pointed to by s1 and which are not found in the string s2.

Prototype: `size_t strcspn(const char *s1,constchar`
                     `*s2);`

Include file: `string.h`

Related functions: `strspn(), strchr(), strstr(), strpbrk()`

Returns: Number of characters at the beginning of string s1 not in s2, or 0 if the first letter of s1 is in s2.

For example,

```
#include <stdio.h>
#include <string.h>

char fststring[80] = "ANSI C Standard";
char sndstring[80] = "C";
int result = 0;
```

```
void main(void)
      {
      result = strcspn(fststring, sndstring);
      printf("The no. of chars = %d\n", result);
      }
```

would print

`"The no. of chars = 5"`.

strerror()

`strerror` gets an error message corresponding to the `errnum` (error number) given as a parameter. The error string should not be modified by your program. It is usually based on system error messages and is compiler- or operating-system-dependent.

Prototype: `char *strerror(int errnum);`

Include file: `string.h`

Related functions: `ferror()`, `perror()`

Returns: Pointer to an error-message string

strlen()

This function returns the length of the string pointed to by s and does not include the null terminator. Because C has no byte associated with a string that holds length information, a function must be used to get the data.

Prototype: `size_t strlen(const char *s);`

Include file: `string.h`

Related functions: `strcmp()`, `strncmp()`

Returns: Size of the string

strncat()

The function `strncat` performs much like `strcat`, except that only n number of characters are concatenated (appended) onto the end of string s1. Again, s1 should be long enough to hold all the

19

characters in it plus those added from string s2, or problems could occur. If n is less then the length of s2, then the remaining characters are not added to s1, and if n is larger than the length of s2, no more characters past the null terminator are added.

Prototype: `char *strncat(char *s1, const char *s2, size_t n);`

Include file: `string.h`

Related functions: `strcat(), strchr(), strcpy(), strncpy()`

Returns: Character pointer to string s1

strncmp()

This function is similar to `strcmp` in that it compares two strings, s1 and s2, for a count of n characters to see whether they differ.

Prototype: `int strncmp(const unsigned char *s1, const unsigned char *s2, size_t n);`

Include file: `string.h`

Related functions: `strcmp(), memcmp()`

Returns: 0 if s1=s2
integer > 0 if s1 > s2
integer < 0 if s1 < s2

strncpy()

The function `strncpy` performs similar to `strcpy`, except that n number of characters are copied from s2 to s1. If, however, there are not n characters in s2, then s1 is padded with spaces up to n characters; and if there are more than n characters in s2, then they are omitted. Again, unpredictable results may occur if s2 and s1 overlap in memory.

Prototype: `char strncpy(char *s1, const char *s2, size_t n);`

Include file: `string.h`

Related functions: `strcpy(), memcpy(), memmove()`

Returns: Character pointer to s1

19

strpbrk()

The function strpbrk searches string s1 for the first occurrence of any character found in the string pointed to by s2. strpbrk is thus a "mini-parser."

Prototype: char *strpbrk(const char *s1, const char *s2);

Include file: string.h

Related functions: strspn(), strcspn(), strchr(), strstr() of s2 that is in s1

Returns: Character pointer to the first character of s2 that is in s1

strrchr()

The function strrchr searches the string s for the *last* occurrence of the character c within the string and returns a pointer to that location.

Prototype: char *strrchr(const char *s, int c);

Include file: string.h

Related functions: strchr(), strstr(), strspn(), strcspn()

Returns: Pointer to the character if found or a null pointer otherwise

strspn()

This function is the opposite of strcspn. strspn calculates the number of characters starting from the beginning of the string pointed to by s1 and which *are* all found in the string s2.

Prototype: size_t strspn(const char *s1, const char *s2);

Include file: string.h

Related functions: strchr(), strstr(), strcspn(), strrchr()

Returns: Number of characters at the beginning of string s1 that are in s2, or 0 if none of s2 is found in s1

19

For example,

```
#include <stdio.h>
#include <string.h>

char fststring[80] = "ANSI C Standard";
char sndstring[80] = "ANSI";
size_t result = 0;

void main(void)
    {

result =   strspn(fststring, sndstring);
           printf("The no. of chars = %d\n", result);
    }
```

would print

```
"The no. of chars = 4".
```

strstr()

The function strstr searches the string s1 for the substring of s2 (the entire string, not just individual characters), so it too acts as a "parser."

Prototype: `char *strstr(const char *s1, const char *s2);`

Include file: `string.h`

Related functions: `strchr(), strrchr(), strspn(), strcspn()`

Returns: Pointer to the beginning of s1 where the characters are found, or a null pointer if not found

strtok()

This function can be used in repeated calls to break the string s1 into tokens delimited by s2. After calling strtok the first time, use NULL instead of s1. The string of delimiters (s2) may be different from call to call or the same. When tokens are found in the string s1, they are removed before the next call to strtok.

Prototype: `char *strtok(char *s1, const char *s2);`

Include file: string.h

Related functions: strchr(), strrchr(), strspn(), strcspn(), strstr()

Returns: Pointer to the token, or a null pointer if there is no token

For example,

```
#include <stdio.h>
#include <string.h>

char fststr[80] = "$9,1832.32 and more";
char sndstr[80] = "$,. ";
char *token;

void main(void)
    {
    token = strtok(fststr, sndstr);
    printf("Token = %s\n", token);
    while (token != NULL)
        {
        token = strtok(NULL, sndstr);
        if (token != NULL)
            printf("Token = %s\n", token);
        }
    }
```

causes the following output:

```
Token = 9
Token = 1832
Token = 32
Token = and
Token = more.
```

strxfrm()

This function changes the string s2 and puts the result into s1, working on n number of characters during the change. It takes locale-specific information (that is, foreign languages, nationalities, and so on) into account during the transformation. The ANSI standard has thought strcoll would be used for those processes requiring a relatively small number of comparisons, saving larger tasks to strxfrm.

19

Prototype: `size_t strxfrm(char *s1, const char *s2, size_t n);`

Include file: `string.h`

Related functions: `strcmp(), strncmp()`

Partner functions: `strcoll()`

Returns: Length of the transformed string (without the null terminator) pointed to by `s1`

Locale-specific Functions— locale.h

struct lconv()

The *locale structure* contains members for formatting numbers for various nationalities, foreign languages, and so on. Table 19.8 lists the contents of the locale structure.

Table 19.8. Contents of the locale structure.

Member	*Meaning*
`char *decimal_point;`	Decimal point for nonmonetary values
`char *thousands_sep;`	Thousands separator for nonmonetary values
`char *grouping;`	String showing the size of groups of digits in nonmonetary values
`char *int_curr_symbol;`	The international currency symbol of up to four characters
`char *currency_symbol;`	Local currency symbol
`char *mon_decimal_point;`	Decimal point for monetary values

Member	Meaning
`char *mon_thousands_sep;`	Separator for thousands in monetary values
`char *mon_grouping;`	String showing the size of groups of digits in monetary values
`char *positive_sign;`	Symbol for positive sign
`char *negative_sign;`	Symbol for negative sign
`char frac_digits;`	Number of digits displayed to the right of the decimal position in monetary quantities
`char p_cs_precedes;`	1 if the currency symbol precedes the monetary value, 0 if after it
`char p_sep_by_space;`	1 if the currency symbol is separated by a space from the monetary value, 0 if not
`char n_cs_precedes;`	1 if the currency symbol precedes the negative monetary value, 0 if not
`char n_sep_by_space;`	1 if the currency symbol is separated by a space from a negative monetary value, 0 if not
`char p_sign_posn;`	Indicates the position of the positive sign for a monetary value
`char n_sign_posn;`	Indicates the position of the negative sign for a monetary value

19

p_sign_posn and n_sign_posn may also have the following values:

    0 = parentheses around the quantity

    1 = sign string precedes the quantity

    2 = sign string succeeds the quantity

    3 = sign string immediately precedes the currency symbol

    4 = sign string immediately succeeds the currency symbol

localeconv()

This function supplies information for filling in the locale structure for numeric values. When the structure is set, it may not be changed by the program unless further calls to localeconv or setlocale are made.

Prototype: `struct lconv *localeconv(void);`

Include file: `locale.h`

Related functions: `setlocale()`

Returns: Pointer to the structure filled in with the appropriate values from the locale information

For example:

U.S. monetary values normally appear as $1,328.59, but the same numbers (not value) formatted for West Germany would be 1.328,59DM. In particular, the mon_decimal_point, mon_thousands_sep, p_cs_precedes, currency_symbol, and perhaps frac_digits, n_sign_posn, and n_cs_precedes values would be set for this example.

setlocale()

The locale parameter can take the values "C" for the minimum requirements for the C language, and an empty string ("") allows use of the compiler-specific environment. Other compiler-specific values are allowed. The function is used to find out parts or the entire package of information for the locale.

Prototype: `char *setlocale(int category,`
`                             const char *locale);`

Include file: `locale.h`

Related functions: `localeconv()`, `strcoll()`, `strxfrm()`, `strftime()`

Returns: String to the category for the new locale, or a null pointer if it cannot be applied

The first parameter `category` can be specified by the following six macros found in `locale.h`:

  `LC_ALL` program's entire locale

  `LC_COLLATE` settings for the `strcoll` and `strxfrm` functions

  `LC_CTYPE` sets actions of character handling functions

  `LC_MONETARY` refers to monetary values

  `LC_NUMERIC` refers to non-monetary numeric values

  `LC_TIME` affects the `strftime` function

Mathematical Functions— math.h

acos()

The function acos calculates the arc cosine of x, which must be in the range of −1 to 1. The result is in radians.

Prototype: `double acos(double x);`

Include file: `math.h`

Related functions: `cos()`, `cosh()`, `asin()`, `atan()`

Returns: Double-precision value for x

asin()

This function calculates the arc sine of x, which must be in the range of −1 to 1. The result is in radians.

Prototype: `double asin(double x);`

Include file: `math.h`

Related functions: `sin()`, `sinh()`, `acos()`, `atan()`

Returns: Double-precision value occurs if x is negative.

atan()

Calculates the arc tangent of x, which must be in the range −1 to 1, and returns the result in radians.

Prototype: `double atan(double x);`

Include file: `math.h`

Related functions: `tan()`, `tanh()`, `acos()`, `asin()`

Returns: Double-precision value for x

atan2()

The function `atan2()` calculates the arc tangent of y and x of the value y/x and returns the result in radians.

Prototype: `double atan2(double y, double x);`

Include file: `math.h`

Related functions: `tan()`, `tanh()`, `atan()`, `acos()`, `asin()`

Returns: Double-precision value for y/x

ceil()

Returns the smallest integer (as a double) that is greater than x.

Prototype: `double ceil(double x);`

Include file: `math.h`

Related functions: `floor()`, `fmod()`

Returns: Double-precision value

cos()

Calculates the cosine of x, which is represented in radians.

Prototype: `double cos(double x);`

Include file: `math.h`

Related functions: `cosh()`, `acos()`

Returns: Double-precision value of x

cosh()

The function `cosh()` calculates the hyperbolic cosine value of x, which is expresed in radians.

Prototype: `double cosh(double x);`

Include file: `math.h`

Related functions: `cos()`, `acos()`

Returns: Double-precision value of x

exp()

Calculates e raised to the xth power.

Prototype: `double exp(double x);`

Include file: `math.h`

Related functions: `log()`

Returns: Double-precision value of x

fabs()

Returns the absolute value of x.

Prototype: `double fabs(double x);`

Include file: `math.h`

Related functions: `abs()`

Returns: Double-precision value of x

floor()

Returns the smallest integer value less than x.

Prototype: `double floor(double x);`

Include file: `math.h`

Related functions: `ceil(), fmod()`

Returns: Double-precision value of x

fmod()

Returns x modulo y.

Prototype: `double fmod(double x, double y);`

Include file: `math.h`

Related functions: `ceil(), floor()`

Returns: Double-precision value of x/y

frexp()

This function calculates the mantissa of `value` so that it is in the range of 0.5 to 1. The function also calculates an integer so that the mantissa times 2 raised to the power of `exp` equals `value` (`value = mantissa * 2^exp`).

Prototype: `double frexp(double value, int *exp);`

Include file: `math.h`

Related functions: `ldexp(), modf()`

Returns: Double-precision value of the mantissa

19

ldexp()

Returns x after calculating x * 2^exp.

Prototype: `double ldexp(double x, int exp);`

Include file: `math.h`

Related functions: `frexp(), modf()`

Returns: Double-precision value of x as calculated

log()

Returns the natural log of x, which must be positive.

Prototype: `double log(double x);`

Include file: `math.h`

Related functions: `exp(), log10()`

Returns: Double-precision value

log10()

Computes the base 10 log of x; an error may occur if x is negative.

Prototype: `double log10(double x);`

Include file: `math.h`

Related functions: `log(), exp()`

Returns: Double-precision base 10 logarithm of x

modf()

The function modf calculates the fractional portion of value and returns it as the result of the function. modf places the integer portion of value into iptr so that it can be obtained also. Do not let the name bother you; it is *not* a modulus function.

Prototype: `double modf(double value, double *iptr);`

Include file: `math.h`

19

Related functions: `frexp()`, `ldexp()`

Returns: Fractional portion of `value`

For example:

If `value` = 32.158, then the result of `modf` would be 0.158, and 32.0 would be stored in `iptr`.

pow()

This function calculates the value of x raised to the power of y (xy). If either x or y is 0, then the result is 0. If either are negative, other errors may occur.

Prototype: `double pow(double x, double y);`

Include file: `math.h`

Related functions: `sqrt()`

Returns: Power as a double-precision value

sin()

`sin()` calculates the sine of x in radians.

Prototype: `double sin(double x);`

Include file: `math.h`

Related functions: `sinh()`, `cosin()`, `cosinh()`

Returns: Double-precision value of x

sinh()

The function `sinh` calculates the hyperbolic sine of x in radians and returns it.

Prototype: `double sinh(double x);`

Include file: `math.h`

Related functions: `sin()`, `cosin()`, `cosinh()`

Returns: Double-precision value of x

sqrt()

This function calculates the square root of x and returns it without error as long as x is not negative.

Prototype: `double sqrt(double x);`

Include file: `math.h`

Related functions: `pow()`

Returns: Double-precision value of x

tan()

The function tan calculates the tangent of x in radians and returns the value.

Prototype: `double tan(double x);`

Include file: `math.h`

Related functions: `tanh()`, `atan()`, `atanh()`

Returns: Double-precision value of x

tanh()

This function calculates the hyperbolic tangent of x in radians.

Prototype: `double tanh(double x);`

Include file: `math.h`

Related functions: `tan()`, `atan()`, `atanh()`

Returns: Double-precision value of x

Time and Date Functions—time.h

struct tm

`struct tm` is a data structure that holds time information. Table 19.9 shows the members of `struct tm`.

Table 19.9. Contents of the time structure.

Member	Meaning
int tm_sec;	Seconds, 0-60. This is to account for a leap second, which is sometimes added at the end of a calendar quarter.
int tm_min;	Minutes
int tm_hour;	Hours, 0-23
int tm_day;	Day of the month, 1-31
int tm_mon;	Month
int tm_year;	Year from 1900
int tm_wday;	Weekday (Sunday=0)
int tm_yday;	Day of the year, 0-365
int tm_isdst;	Daylight saving time flag

All value ranges except the day of the month start with 0. The daylight saving time flag has three values: positive if in effect, zero (0) if not in effect, or negative if information not available.

asctime()

This function changes the time into a string of the following form:

```
Tue Feb 25 11:21:35 1988\n\0
```

The string should be placed elsewhere or printed before making another call to the function.

Prototype: `char *asctime(const struct tm *timeptr);`

Include file: `time.h`

Related functions: `ctime()`, `time()`

Returns: Pointer to the time represented as a string

clock()

This function determines the processor time used since the start of the program, if possible.

Prototype: `clock_t clock(void);`

Include file: `time.h`

Related functions: `asctime(), ctime(), time()`

Partner functions: `macro(), CLK_TCK()`

Returns: Processor time used, which can be changed to seconds by dividing the value by the macro `CLK_TCK`; or −1 cast to the type `clock_t` if the time is not available

ctime()

Creates the same 26-character string as `asctime` but can take the time value from the routine `time` directly.

Prototype: `char *ctime(const time_t *timer);`

Include file: `time.h`

Related functions: `time(), asctime()`

Returns: Character pointer to time represented as a string

difftime()

The function `difftime` merely calculates the difference between `time1` and `time0` and reports it in seconds.

Prototype: `double difftime(time_t time1, time_t time0);`

Include file: `time.h`

Related functions: `time(), gmtime(), localtime(), asctime()`

Returns: Time in seconds

gmtime()

This function converts the time into Greenwich Mean Time and stores the information.

Prototype: `struct tm *gmtime(const time_t *timer);`

Include file: `time.h`

19

Related functions: `localtime()`, `ctime()`, `asctime()`, `time()`

Returns: Pointer to data structure holding time information, or null pointer on error

localtime()

The function `localtime` converts time information into local time, which may include converting according to daylight saving time or the local time zone.

Prototype: `struct tm *localtime(const time_t *timer);`

Include file: `time.h`

Related functions: `gmtime()`, `ctime()`, `asctime()`, `time()` information, or null pointer on error

Returns: Pointer to data structure holding time information, or null pointer on error.

mktime()

`mktime` changes the information in the structure pointed to by `timeptr` into calendar time. The day of the week (`tm_wday`) and day of the year (`tm_yday`) values are ignored during conversion, and the ranges may be different.

Prototype: `time_t mktime(struct tm *timeptr);`

Include file: `time.h`

Related functions: `ctime()`, `asctime()`, `time()`

Returns: Calendar time, or −1 if not available

strftime()

This function, "string format time," puts time information as formatted by `format` and places no more than `maxsize` number of characters into the string `s`. The formatting is similar to that used with functions such as `printf`. Table 19.10 gives the most common formatting characters.

Prototype: `size_t strftime(char *s, size_t maxsize,const char *format, const struct tm *timeptr);`

Include file: `time.h`

Related functions: `time()`, `gmtime()`, `localtime()`

Returns: Number of characters placed into s not including the terminating null character if the total number of characters is less than `maxsize`; otherwise 0

Table 19.10. Common string format characters for time functions.

Character	Meaning
%a	abbreviated weekday name
%A	full name of the weekday
%b	abbreviated month name
%B	full name of the month
%c	locale's date and time representation
%d	day of the month (1-31)
%H	hour of the day (0-23); 24-hour clock basis
%I	hour of the day (1-12); 12-hour clock basis
%j	day of the year (1-366)
%m	month of the year (1-12)
%M	minute (0-59)
%p	locale's version of AM or PM
%S	seconds (0-59)
%U	week number of the year (0-53) with Sunday as the first day of the week
%w	weekday (Sunday=0 to Saturday=6)
%W	week number of the year (0-53) with Monday as the first day of the week

continues

Table 19.10. continued

Character	Meaning
%x	locale's date representation (that is, mm/dd/yy or dd/mm/yy)
%X	locale's time representation
%y	two-digit year representation (00-99)
%Y	year with century (for example, 1988)
%Z	time zone name
%%	percent sign (%)

time()

The function time gets the calendar time from the system; it also may assign the time to whatever timer points to if it is not NULL. It is often used in conjunction with randomizing routines for seeding them.

Prototype: time_t time(time_t *timer);

Include file: time.h

Related functions: asctime(), ctime()

Returns: Time as calendar time; non-ANSI forms may return the time as long values

General Utilities—stdlib.h

abort()

This function makes a program terminate as the cause of a hardware problem or by executing something illegally. Program termination can be prevented if the signal SIGABRT is processed. It does not return anything.

Prototype: void abort(void);

Include file: `stdlib.h`

Partner functions: `signal()`

Related functions: `atexit(), exit()`

Returns: None

abs()

abs calculates and returns the absolute value of j. For example, if

`j = -34`

then

`abs returns 34.`

Prototype: `int abs(int j);`

Include file: `stdlib.h`

Related functions: `labs()`

Returns: Integer value of j

atexit()

atexit registers the function passed as a parameter, with a minimum of 32 functions. These functions will be called at program termination.

Prototype: `int atexit(void (*func) (void));`

Include file: `stdlib.h`

Related functions: `abort(), signal()`

Partner functions: `exit()`

Returns: Zero (0) if function registration succeeds, or a nonzero value if not

atof()

The function atof takes a number in the form of a string pointed to by nptr and converts it into a double-precision floating point

19

number for further use. It has been included in the C Draft Standard for compatibility with UNIX and other systems.

Prototype: `double atof(const char *nptr);`

Include file: `stdlib.h`

Related functions: `atoi()`, `atol()`

Returns: Double-precision value after conversion; most compilers return 0 if the string is not valid.

For example:

```
double result;
result = atof("2937.382");
```

atoi()

`atoi` converts a number in the form of a string to an integer value, where the string must be in the form of a valid integer.

Prototype: `int atoi(const char *nptr);`

Include file: `stdlib.h`

Related functions: `atof()`, `atol()`

Returns: Integer value of string after conversion; most compilers return 0 if the string is not valid.

For example:

```
int result;
result = atoi("392");
```

atol()

`atol` converts a number in the form of a string to a long integer value, where the string must be in the form of a valid integer.

Prototype: `long int atol(const char *nptr);`

Include file: `stdlib.h`

Related functions: `atof()`, `atoi()`

19

Returns: Long integer value of string after conversion; most compilers return 0 if the string is not valid.

For example:

```
long result;
result = atol("299388828");
```

bsearch()

The lengthy function call for bsearch provides a generic binary search routine for C. A sorted object, such as an array, is given to the function in base, and the routine searches for a member as specified in key. The object is composed of nmemb number of members, each of size size.

A comparison function is supplied by int (*compar), which requires two arguments. They are compared, and the function returns one of the following:

◆ An integer < 0 if the key is > *member

◆ 0 if the key matches *member

◆ An integer > 0 if the key is < *member

In other words, if we search an integer array consisting of 1-10 and the key = 4, then comparing 4 with 1-3 would return −1 or a value < 0; comparing the key of 4 with 4 would return 0; and comparing the key of 4 with 5-10 would return 1 or a value greater than 0.

Prototype:
```
void *bsearch(const void *key,
              const void *base, size_t
              nmemb, size_t size, int
              (*compar) (const void *,
              const void *));
```

Include file: stdlib.h

Related functions: qsort()

Returns: Void pointer (generic) to the matching member, or a null pointer if no match occurs

19

For example:

```
#include <stdio.h>
#include <string.h>
#include <stdlib.h>   /* or #include <alloc.h> in some */

static char *stringarr[] ={"Ann ", "Bob ", "Frank",
                           "Jack", "Steve"};
int arrelem = 5;
/* add one to length of the string for null char  */
int lenstr = strlen(stringarr[2] + 1);

/* function to compare two strings for use in bsearch */
int comparestrings(char *string1, char *string2)
    {
    return(strncmp(string1, string2, strlen(string1)));
    }

void main(void)
    {
    char *result;
    char *member;
    int i;

    member = (char *)malloc(lenstr);
    result = (char*)malloc(lenstr);
    member = "Jack ";

    /*  search for the member in the array using
        bsearch */
    result =(char *)bsearch(member, stringarr[0],
            arrelem, lenstr, comparestrings);

    printf("Result = %s\n", result);
    if (result)
        printf("The value %s was found.\n", member);
    else
        printf("The value was not found.\n");
    }
```

This example uses bsearch to perform a binary search for the name "Jack" within stringarr. It displays the name and a message.

19

calloc()

This function creates storage in memory (on the heap) for nmemb number of items, each of size bytes in size. It also initializes each byte set aside with 0 (that is, all bits are set to 0), so it wipes out any existing values or garbage present in memory. The sizeof operator normally is used to determine the number of bytes to set aside. The return from calloc, malloc, or realloc should always be checked for a NULL pointer, which means not enough memory was available or some other problem occurred.

Prototype: void *calloc(size_t nmemb, size_t size); (char *calloc() in non-ANSI forms)

Include file: stdlib.h—(m)alloc.h in non-ANSI compilers

Related functions: malloc(), realloc()

Partner functions: free()

Returns: Void (generic) pointer for use by other functions; older versions usually use a cast (char *) to change the result of the memory management functions. A null pointer is returned on error, such as in cases where not enough memory is available.

For example,

```
struct bookreference *thisBook;
if ((thisBook = (struct bookreference *)calloc(10,
    sizeof(struct bookreference))) == NULL)
    printf("Problem allocating memory\n");
```

would set aside memory for 10 structures of the same size as the struct bookreference and set all memory locations to 0.

div()

This function calculates the quotient and remainder portions of numer/denom and returns them. div_t is defined in stdlib.h.

Prototype: div_t div(int numer, int denom);

Include file: stdlib.h

Related functions: ldiv()

19

Returns: Quotient and remainder portions

exit()

The function exit causes a program to terminate due to some error condition; but before termination, the functions previously registered by atexit are called and executed in reverse order. Objects with automatic storage (local) should not be used or the results are unknown. Also, all open streams (files) are flushed, closed, and any files created by the function tmpfile are deleted. Then, control is returned to the system.

Prototype: `void exit(int status);`

Include file: `stdlib.h`

Related functions: `abort(), signal()`

Partner functions: `atexit()`

Returns: None

free()

The function free returns memory back to the system that was previously allocated by malloc, calloc, or realloc. If ptr is a null pointer, then no action is performed. Memory is not returned to the system until the process that allocated it is terminated, or unless free is used. Failure to allocate memory and not release it results in not being able to execute further when the memory is exhausted. Many systems provide another function, cfree, specifically to release the memory allocated by calloc, but it is not part of the ANSI C Draft Standard.

Prototype: `void free(void *ptr);`

Include file: `stdlib.h`—(m)`alloc.h` in non-ANSI compilers

Related functions: None

Partner functions: `malloc(), calloc(), realloc()`

Returns: None

19

getenv()

This function retrieves environmental information depending on the implementation. The string returned cannot be modified by the program. `getenv` would get the DOS environment information in PC compilers (path, set variables, and so on).

Prototype: `char *getenv(const char *name);`

Include file: `stdlib.h`

Related functions: `system()`

Returns: Pointer to environment information if found, or else a null pointer

labs()

The function `labs` calculates and returns the absolute value of `j`.

Prototype: `long int labs(long int j);`

Include file: `stdlib.h`

Related functions: `abs()`

Returns: Long integer value

ldiv()

This function calculates the result of `numer/denom` and returns both the quotient and remainder as the type `ldiv_t`.

Prototype: `ldiv_t ldiv(long int numer, long int denom);`

Include file: `stdlib.h`

Related functions: `div()`

Returns: Long integer values of the quotient and remainder

malloc()

`malloc` is the most commonly used allocation function. It sets aside storage for an object of size `size` and returns a pointer to the beginning of that location on the heap. The function `free` should be used to release the memory when finished. It does not set the memory to any particular value. The return from `calloc`, `malloc`, or `realloc` should always be checked for a NULL pointer, which means not enough memory was available or that some other problem occurred. Many systems use `char *malloc()`.

Prototype: `void *malloc(size_t size);`

Include file: `stdlib.h`—(m)alloc.h in non-ANSI compilers

Related functions: `calloc()`, `realloc()`

Partner functions: `free()`

Returns: Void pointer to the section of memory just allocated, or a null pointer if no memory is available

mblen()

This function is for handling multibyte characters to be used in applications. This refers to languages such as Japanese and Chinese, where the number of characters (there are thousands!) in a language exceeds the one-byte-per-character rule. It is the equivalent of `strlen` in that it calculates the number of bytes in the character pointed to by s. No more than n characters are viewed.

Prototype: `int mblen(const char *s, size_t n);`

Include file: `stdlib.h`

Related functions: `mbtowc()`, `wctomb()`, `mbstowcs()`, `strlen()`

Returns: If s is a null pointer, the function returns one of the following:

◆ A nonzero value if there are state-dependent encodings

◆ A 0 if the encodings are absent

If s is not a null pointer, the function returns one of the following:

◆ 0 if s points to a null character

◆ The number of bytes making up a valid multibyte character

◆ −1 if the character is not valid

19

mbstowcs()

This function examines n number of multibyte characters starting with the one pointed to by s and converts them into the appropriate codes, which are then stored in pwcs. The shift state of the characters is not affected.

Prototype: `size_t mbstowcs(wchar_t *pwcs,`
`                    const char *s, size_t n);`

Include file: `stdlib.h`

Related functions: `mblen(), wctomb(), mbtowc(),`
`wcstombs()`

Returns: −1 is returned if the character is invalid, otherwise the number of members that are converted is returned

mbtowc()

The function `mbtowc` first calculates the number of bytes in the multibyte character found in s, then the code for its value is determined. The encodings deal with various shift states the character enters as it is used. If the code is valid and pwc is not a null pointer, then the function places the code in pwc. No more than n characters are taken into consideration.

Prototype: `int mbtowc(wchar_t *pwc, const char *s,`
`            size_t n);`

Include file: `stdlib.h`

Related functions: `mblen(), wctomb(), mbstowcs()`

Returns: If s is a null pointer, the function returns one of the following:

◆ A nonzero value if the character has locale-dependent encodings

◆ 0 if the encodings are absent

19

If s is not a null pointer, the function returns one of the following:

◆ 0 if s points to a null character

◆ The number of bytes in the valid character

◆ −1 if the character is not valid

qsort()

This function implements a generic "quicksort" (one of the fastest sorts) routine in C. base points to the beginning of the object (array, etc.) to be sorted in ascending order, which consists of nmemb members, each of size size. The function pointer points to a function that compares the two pointers given as parameters in the declaration and which returns one of the following:

◆ An integer < 0 if the key is > *member

◆ 0 if the key matches *member

◆ An integer > 0 if the key is < *member

In other words, if we search an integer array consisting of 1-10 and the key = 4, then comparing 4 with 1-3 would return −1 or a value < 0; comparing the key of 4 with 4 would return 0; and comparing the key of 4 with 5-10 would return 1 or a value greater than 0. It could be performed before doing bsearch, for instance.

Prototype:
```
void qsort(void *base, size_t nmemb,
           size_t size, int (*compar)
           (const void *, const void *));
```

Include file: stdlib.h

Related functions: bsearch()

Returns: None

For example:

```
#include <stdio.h>
#include <string.h>
#include <stdlib.h>
```

19

```
static char *stringarr[] ={"Bob  ", "Jack ", "Frank",
                           "Steve", "Ann  "};
int arrelem = 5;
/*  add one to length of the string for null char   */
int lenstr = strlen(stringarr[2] + 1);

/*  function to compare two strings for use in qsort */
int comparestrings(char *string1, char *string2)
    {
    return(strcmp(string1, string2));
    }

void main(void)
    {
    int i;

    /*  sort the array using qsort   */
    qsort(stringarr[0], arrelem, lenstr,
          comparestrings);

    printf("The sorted list:\n\n");
    for (count = 0; count < arrelem; ++count)
        printf("%s\n", stringarr[count]);
    }
```

This example uses qsort() as a fast sorting method to place the array of names stringarr in alphabetical order. The names are then displayed on the screen.

rand()

This function is used as a pseudo-random number generator for such applications as statistics, protection schemes, real-life simulation, etc. The generator should first be seeded (initialized) using srand. Using the same seed (or without calling srand), rand generates the same series of random numbers with each call. rand can be used as rand() % number to determine a number within the range of 0 to number-1.

Prototype: int rand(void);

Include file: stdlib.h

Related functions: None

Partner functions: srand()

Returns: Integer in the range of 0 to (in ANSI C) RAND_MAX, which is 32767. But some compilers may use a higher upper limit, such as the upper limit for a long int.

For example,

```
long presentTime;
  int count;

void main(void)
    {
    srand(time(&presentTime));

    for (count = 0; count < 5; count++)
        printf("Number %2d = %6d\n", count, rand());
    }
```

would result in output similar to the following:

```
Number  0 =   21599
Number  1 =   25210
Number  2 =    5883
Number  3 =   21745
Number  4 =     583
```

realloc()

The function realloc resizes to the new size size the memory set aside by a prior call to malloc or calloc. The contents of the memory are not corrupted. If space is not available (when more is needed) at the present location, then a new location may be selected, the contents copied there, and a new pointer returned.

If the size requested is smaller than the memory location, the end of the contents will be truncated. ptr is a pointer to a memory location from either malloc or calloc. prt is useful when a dynamic structure (union, struct) has been put into memory along with another structure after it. If the first structure must grow, then realloc can be used to help provide extra room or obtain a new location if memory exists. The return from calloc, malloc, or realloc should always be checked for a NULL pointer, which means not enough memory was available or some other problem occurred.

19

Prototype: `void *realloc(void *ptr, size_t size);`

Include file: `stdlib.h`—`(m)alloc.h` in non-ANSI compilers

Related functions: `malloc()`, `calloc()`

Partner functions: `free()`

Returns: Void pointer to the memory just allocated, or a null pointer if no memory is available

srand()

The function `srand` initializes the pseudorandom-number generator, and a different `seed` produces a different series of random numbers. The `seed` is often a result of using some form of the `time` or a system time function. See `rand` for an example.

Prototype: `void srand(unsigned int seed);`

Include file: `stdlib.h`

Related functions: None

Partner functions: `rand()`

Returns: None

strtod()

This function changes a string, `nptr`, into a double precision value by first stripping out any leading whitespace characters, then continuing until it finds any character which is not a part of a valid floating point number (valid characters include E, e, -, +, ., and the digits 0-9). In other words, the string given as a parameter to `strtod` does not have to consist of only a valid number but can include other text as well. When finished, the pointer `endptr` points to the character after the last valid character of the number. Octal and decimal constant formats are also allowed.

Prototype: `double strtod(const char *nptr,`
`                     char **endptr);`

Include file: `stdlib.h`

19

Related functions: `strtol()`, `strtoul()`

Returns: Double-precision value of converted string, or 0 if not valid or if problems occur

strtol()

The function `strtol` also converts a number to a long integer value, using the string `nptr`. The last parameter, `base`, refers to the radix of the number: if it is 0, then an octal, a decimal, or a hexidecimal constant is expected, but other values ranging from 2 to 36 are allowed. The pointer `endptr` signifies the position of the first nonvalid character in the input string.

Prototype:
```
long int strtol(const char *nptr,
                char **endptr, int base);
```

Include file: `stdlib.h`

Related functions: `strtod()`, `strtoul()`

Returns: Converted string as a long integer value, or 0 if not valid or on error

strtoul()

The function `strtoul` converts a number to an unsigned long integer value, using the string `nptr`. The last parameter, `base`, refers to the radix of the number; if it is 0, then an octal, a decimal, or a hexidecimal constant is expected, but other values ranging from 2 to 36 are allowed. The pointer `endptr` signifies the position of the first nonvalid character in the input string. A minus sign (–) or plus sign (+) may not be used as part of the number.

Prototype:
```
unsigned long int strtoul(const char *nptr,
                          char **endptr,
                          int base);
```

Include file: `stdlib.h`

Related functions: `strtod()`, `strtol()`

Returns: Converted string as an unsigned long integer value, or 0 if not valid or on error

19

system()

The function system hands the string over to the host operating system or environment for execution. It is useful for performing system commands under DOS (for example, backup, restore, delete, etc.) and returning to the program.

Prototype: `int system(const char *string);`

Include file: `stdlib.h`

Related functions: `getenv(), interrupts()`

Returns: If the parameter is a null pointer, a nonzero value is returned *only* if a command processor is available; an implementation-defined value is returned otherwise.

For example:

```
system("cd c:\prog\data");
```

wcstombs()

The function wcstombs looks at no more than n number of multibyte characters from the location starting with pwcs and stores them in s as multibyte characters in their beginning shift state.

Prototype: `size_t wcstombs(char *s, const`
                    `wchar_t *pwcs, size_t n);`

Include file: `stdlib.h`

Related functions: `mblen(), wctomb(), mbtowc(), mbstowcs()`

Returns: If s is a null pointer, the function returns one of the following:

◆ A nonzero value if the character has locale-dependent encodings

◆ 0 if the encodings are absent

19

If s is not a null pointer, the function returns one of the following:

◆ 0 if s points to a null character

◆ The number of bytes in the valid multibyte character

◆ −1 if the character is not valid

wctomb()

This function calculates the number of bytes required to hold the character whose code is in wchar. The multibyte character is stored in s.

Prototype: `int wctomb(char *s, wchar_t wchar);`

Include file: `stdlib.h`

Related functions: `mblen()`, `mbtowc()`, `mbstowcs()`, `wcstombs()`

Returns: If s is a null pointer, the function returns one of the following:

◆ A nonzero value if the character has locale-dependent encodings

◆ 0 if the encodings are absent

If s is not a null pointer, the function returns one of the following:

◆ 0 if s points to a null character

◆ The number of bytes in the valid multibyte character

◆ −1 if the character is not valid

Nonlocal Jumps—setjmp.h

longjump()

The function longjmp provides a means of a nonlocal jump (goto) for extraordinary or unusual circumstances. A nonlocal jump is a jump between functions instead of within one function. env must be an array type (of type jmp_buf found in setjmp.h), and this buffer must have obtained its values from a prior call to the